WHAT ABOUT
YOUR SAUCEPANS?

By Lindsay de Feliz

What About Your Saucepans? by Lindsay de Feliz

First published Great Britain 2013 by *Summertime Publishing*

© Copyright Lindsay de Feliz

ISBN 978-1-909193-31-4

Design by Owen Jones Design
www.owenjonesdesign.com

DEDICATION

This book is dedicated to my father, Peter Firth, with whom I only developed a deep relationship during the latter years of his life, when he gave me unwavering love and support. He died swiftly and unexpectedly in 2005. I miss him dreadfully.

To my grandmother, Irene Jones, an inspiration born before her time, who supported me throughout the many changes in my life. She died in 2006 aged 99.

To Ginnie Bedggood, author and great friend. She was my rock when I had my darkest and most difficult moments in the DR, always there to explain how the country worked and helping me make decisions. She died suddenly in 2010.

To my mother, Shirley Firth. There cannot be a more supportive mother anywhere in the world. I love you.

Finally this book is dedicated to Dominicans everywhere. To their joy, their friendliness, their generosity and spirit in overcoming impossible situations every day. Thank you for letting me live in your beautiful country.

ACKNOWLEDGMENTS

I WOULD NOT HAVE SURVIVED THE LAST FEW YEARS, PHYSICALLY, emotionally or financially without the help of many people.

First and foremost my mother. Thank you from the bottom of my heart mum.

My sister, Elisabeth, her husband Gary, and other family who were there when I was desperate.

Shirley, my best friend, who has been online day and night as a constant contact with the outside world, and her husband Charlie, who tragically died of cancer in 2010.

Those who crossed my path, stayed in touch and were there when I needed them most. Heather and Ian, Nicole, Robyn, Perri, John Boyter, Grace, Laura Jane, Pati, Marco and Grahame. Ilana, Yana, Ed and Jonathan for giving me work. And those from my past life who didn't forget me, Nicola, John Paterson, Sue, Annie, Mark Hynes, Creenagh, Cathy and Chris, and Jill.

Special thanks to John Evans for making me laugh every day for the last four years.

A heartfelt thank you to my editor, Jane Dean, who took on this book when I had nowhere else to turn. She has been a joy to work with and somehow turned my ramblings into a real book.

And thanks to my publisher, Jo Parfitt at Summertime Publishing for setting me on the right path and whose incredible insight made the manuscript work. I had no idea so much was involved.

Finally Danilo. My man from Barahona who took me with him into unchartered waters. Sometimes calm and sometimes so rough I doubted I would survive. You taught me about the strength of the human spirit and I learnt that with optimism and faith we can cope with anything. I adore you and always will.

TABLE OF CONTENTS

WHAT ABOUT YOUR SAUCEPANS?

CHAPTER ONE
IN SEARCH OF A DREAM

I BLAME *COSMOPOLITAN* MAGAZINE FOR THE DECISION THAT kick-started the major changes in my life. In fact, I think *Cosmo* has a lot to answer for in respect to decisions women have made throughout the years. For my part, I was living in Ormskirk, Lancashire, had been working for a major insurance company in Liverpool for nine or ten years, had my own house, a sports car and earned a reasonable salary. I was thirty years old, single, fun loving, a hardworking career woman, but had a nagging feeling something was missing in my life.

I was sitting at the dining room table one Sunday morning, spring sunshine streaming in through the patio doors, highlighting the patches of dust I had missed on the sideboard. Hot coffee steamed in my favourite blue mug, and smoke curled from a Benson and Hedges, as I flicked through the pages of *Cosmo*. Suddenly something caught my eye. A competition with the opportunity to study for an MBA as the prize. 'Write and submit 500 words as to why you deserve the chance to study for an MBA'. This was 1985. Very few people had an MBA, and even fewer women. *This is your chance*, I thought to myself, *you know you're bright, and if you had an MBA you could get a better job, have a more exciting life, maybe work overseas and you'd have more money*. I had tremendous faith in my own abilities. My plans for the day changed and I spent hours writing my essay, folded it neatly into an envelope and ran down to the post box to mail it in time for the deadline.

Every day I waited anxiously for the postman. Eventually the letter came, but sadly I had not won the competition. Undeterred, I wondered, *Why don't I do it anyway? I could sell the house and use the equity to study for an MBA. Think what fun it would be to be a student again*. So that's what I did.

It wasn't the first time I had let my heart rule my head.

My mother went back to work as a teacher when I was four and as there was no one to look after me, and I could already read, I started school, having no problems keeping up with my older classmates. I clearly remember one incident at school – the first time I acted in haste without thinking through the consequences. This pattern was to repeat itself time and again, resulting in the major turning points in my life.

My teacher asked her young assistant to take the class outside onto the playing field and read us a story. It was a warm, sunny summer's day and we were relieved to be out of the gloomy classroom. There were twenty five-year-olds and me. We sat in a haphazard circle on the soft grass and the assistant began to read. I had heard the story before and without thinking piped up imperiously, "I know that one. I don't want to hear it again. Read me something else."

She was taken aback but hid her surprise, reached for another book and started to read a different story. I folded my arms in disgust at her choice, banged my hands down on my grubby, grass stained knees in annoyance. "I know that one too. Read something new," I demanded, tossing my dark hair out of my eyes.

"Right, I've had enough of you, young lady," she exclaimed. She stood up awkwardly, brushed the bits of dried grass from her crumpled skirt before grabbing my arm tightly and, striding purposefully, marched me back to the classroom.

"You can't do this," I screamed, trying to pull away from her. "My mummy is a teacher here. She'll be cross with you, then you'll be in really big trouble!"

We arrived in the hot, airless classroom and she turned, lifted me up under both arms and sat me down on one of the little wooden chairs.

"Now, you sit right there and be quiet until I have read the good children a story," she ordered, her face flushed with heat and suppressed anger at being told what to do by a four-year-old. "And don't you dare move until I get back!"

I waited until she left and, determined to teach her a lesson, crept over to the cupboard where the drawing materials were kept. It was a small wooden cupboard, about three feet high, with two doors. By moving the wax crayons on top of the paper I could squeeze onto the bottom shelf, and there I waited, all scrunched up. I smiled to myself as I thought of the trouble she would be in when the class came back from story time and I wasn't there.

Story time ended and the children trooped back into the classroom and of course I was nowhere to be seen. Panic ensued, my mother had to leave her class and everyone was looking for me. I remember hearing the student teacher sobbing.

Ha! I thought, *that will teach you.* It struck me perhaps there would not be universal joy when I clambered out of my cupboard. There were two potential outcomes. One was unbounded relief I had not been kidnapped by pirates or the circus. The second was unbridled fury I had caused such concern and upset. What had seemed a good idea at the time was not feeling like that now, and as there was no way I could stay in the cupboard indefinitely, I had to make an appearance. And I was right, I was in trouble and there was no universal joy at the discovery I was still alive. Unfortunately I did not learn from this, and it was exactly the same when I read *Cosmopolitan* magazine. It seemed like a good idea at the time to give up everything I had worked for for ten years, and start all over again.

I loved studying for the MBA. I was one of only four women on the course with over a hundred men, and it was there I met the man who was to become my husband – Steve. It wasn't part of the plan to have a relationship. The plan was to graduate and get a highflying job, travel, maybe live abroad, make lots of money and enjoy life. But one day I was sat in a lecture theatre and someone was talking behind me, annoying me as I tried to concentrate on the lecture. I twisted around.

"Shhh... I'm trying to listen!" I snapped, as I looked at his face, grinning at me. Good looking, short dark hair, a slight resemblence to George Clooney, and by the time I turned back to my notes I was smiling. By coincidence we were both elected as student representatives, so had to spend time together and it wasn't long before we were an item.

Apart from studying for an MBA we had little in common. I was thirty and he was twenty-three. I had been working for nine years and he had been studying to be an architect. I loved spending money and he loved saving it. I had travelled and worked abroad, he had only been to Spain with 'the boys'.

After completing the MBA I began working for a building society in Bradford, where we'd been studying. I loved the north of England, and Steve went back to London to start work. It was a typical long distance relationship, with me doing most of the travelling. I would spend my time looking forward to seeing him but once we were together, there was never the magic I had imagined. It took a day or so for us to feel comfortable with each other and then I had to leave again. I remember once arriving back from a holiday in Greece with my sister, and I had really missed him. When we arrived back at the airport I saw people being met, and, being the eternal romantic, wished someone had been there to meet me, to come running to greet me and give me a big hug.

I phoned Steve and told him I would be flying down to London the following week rather than driving, and spent a fortune on a flight in the hope of realising this dream. The plane landed and I was beside myself with excitement. I knew I looked good – tight blue jeans, high heeled boots to make me look taller and crisp white shirt with a few buttons open to show off the Greek tan.

As I descended on the escalator in terminal one I struck the pose as I saw Steve sitting on the edge of the baggage carousel below. I waited for the scene I had imagined – him running towards me. It didn't happen. He didn't move. As I approached him, crestfallen it wasn't how it was supposed to be, he put up his hand.

"Stop. Don't come any closer. I ate a whole raw onion last night as part of a bet and I stink. But can you hurry up... I want to see the second half of the cup final?" he said. I noticed his eyes did not meet mine.

Nothing ever quite matched up to my dreams of how I thought things should be, although I do realise they were often unrealistic.

Meanwhile I was becoming increasingly frustrated working to make money for other people, and wanted to do something more meaningful. The trigger for change this time? I had been asked to give a talk on personal finance at a local school, aimed at a group of 'problem' children who were academic underachievers.

I stood nervously in front of the students in the dingy assembly hall, looking around at bored, uninterested faces. *Bloody hell this is nerve wracking*, I thought, heart racing and hands sweating as I pulled the foils for the overhead projector out of my briefcase. I took a deep breath to calm my nerves and started.

"Good morning everyone," I began, my voice shaking. The children looked at me blankly and started to mutter amongst themselves. "Okay, who wants to be a millionaire?" I queried, and every hand shot up in the air.

"Right, I'm going to tell you how to do it – legally," I continued, more confidently. As I noticed them smiling and laughing, I felt the adrenaline surge inside me and from then on we had a conversation – me asking questions, wandering amongst them, probing, laughing, joking, and them responding. I loved every minute of it and when the talk was over, I floated on a high back to the car.

"That's what I want to do," I sang to myself. "I want to teach. At last I know what I want to do."

I sold my house, resigned from my job and moved to London, living with Steve in a terraced house he owned, and became a lecturer at Kingston Polytechnic, later to become Kingston University. My salary dropped by a third but I loved the freedom of not having to dress up so much, not working 8am – 6pm each day, and the pleasure I got from helping the personal development of students.

Steve and I married in April 1990, and immediately we started trying to have children. That was when the perfect life started to unravel. Since the beginning of time women have had children, but I couldn't become pregnant. Between us we had graduate degrees, Masters' Degrees, professional qualifications, a house, cars, and a good lifestyle. Yet I could not achieve what most other women could. Steve wasn't so concerned about having children straight away, but I was thirty-five and knew time was running out. I arranged visits to specialists to find out what was wrong and reluctantly he came along. There was nothing wrong with either of us apparently, so the only option was to take fertility drugs, followed by in vitro fertilisation or IVF.

The attempts to have a baby began to take over my life. Every treatment cycle I would travel to central London daily to have blood taken, or for a scan, sitting in a waiting room with pregnant women stroking their swollen bellies, and each time it failed, I never became pregnant. I remember once going to Hammersmith hospital to have blood drawn, and was sent to wait for the nurse in a delivery room. I looked at the equipment and the pain of knowing I would probably never be in a room like that, giving birth to my own child, washed over me like a tidal wave taking my breath away and leaving me devastated.

After five years we gave up trying to conceive and things started to change between us. I tried to talk about it.

"Steve are you happy with the way life is?"

"Yes, of course. My job is fine. We have a great house in London, a cottage in the country... what more could we want?"

"I want to feel happy. I want to **do** something, not just work, come home and watch television, and go on holidays once or twice a year. There must be more to life than this. Why can't we buy a little house in the Caribbean and spend some time there."

"Waste of bloody money. We need to save, not spend. You always want to spend money. And anyway I'm far too busy at work." I felt there had to be some compensation for not being able to have children and if I wasn't going to leave my genes on this earth when I died, I had to leave some remembrance of having been here. What or how wasn't clear.

I had to find something to fill the aching gap so I left lecturing and went back into industry. The 'almost perfect' life continued. Bigger house, better car, designer clothes and more 'things'. I tried to ignore the nagging voices in my head telling me all was not well, something was still missing, but after ten years of marriage, I did it again. This time it was the most enormous change, the craziest, 'It seemed like a good idea at the time' of them all.

A handful of times in my life I had felt pure, unbridled, uplifting joy. It would appear from nowhere; standing on top of a mountain in Wales, driving fast with the roof down on a sunny day, walking on a tropical beach, listening to a thousand Welsh male voices singing at the Royal Albert Hall. You couldn't summon it up. It washed over me like a wave when it happened and then would disappear. I wanted to feel this joy more often. It never happened in London, where I felt more and more like a bird with clipped wings. Unable to do what I wanted, or go where I wanted, I had to conform to the 'norms' and be a good wife and a good worker. Time was rushing by and I could not bear the thought of spending the rest of my life in a gilded cage, with all the trappings of a successful life, but which felt increasingly meaningless.

I had learned to scuba dive, as Steve was a diver and it was something we could do together. Every time I dived I felt intense joy and a rush of exhilaration as I swam effortlessly eighty feet under the ocean with shoals of brightly coloured fish. I went on more diving trips as often as I could, often alone as Steve had to work, and usually to the Maldives where the diving was exquisite. I gave up my sixty hour a week job in the City to become a freelance consultant to spend more time diving, and after a year it still wasn't enough. It was a drug and I wanted more.

The epiphany happened in the Maldives. I was on a live-aboard dive-boat, and one particular night we were barbecuing on a tiny island, not much bigger than a roundabout, in the middle of the Indian Ocean. It was pitch black and the stars were sparkling and glistening like distant diamonds. They went from one horizon all the way to the other. I stood at the edge of the island where the warm ocean lapped against my toes, looking up at the stars and marvelling at the vastness of the universe. I felt an arm come round my shoulders.

"That's your star there. Scorpio." It was one of the Maldivian instructors and he pointed out many of the other stars.

I don't want to live in London anymore a voice in my head screamed! *Why can't I just be here? There can't be anything more wonderful than living here, diving and looking at these stars, night after night.*

Don't be ridiculous, snapped the voice of reason. *You're married. You can't just do what you like.*

Who says I can't? I don't love him anymore anyway. I don't want to be married. I want to be free to do what I want, when I want. I want to enjoy my life, every single day. There, I had done it. I had dared to think it and say it to myself. I didn't love my husband anymore and once I admitted it, there on a sandbank in the middle of the Indian Ocean, the die was cast.

I left my husband of ten years, my job and my country to become a scuba diving instructor. As you do.

No more corporate life, no more working hard to save for some mythical future, I wanted to enjoy life now and what better way than to work in diving, which made me truly happy. Diving, tropical heat, white sandy beaches, swaying palm trees, warm crystalline water. Money had never been that important to me, although nice to have, it was merely a means to an end. The fact I would be earning a fraction of what I had been did not enter my head. It was a selfish decision with no real thought as to where I would go or if I would return. I planned my exit methodically over a six-week period, moving my clothes into a storage locker, sorting bank accounts, insurance, power of attorney for my parents. For the most part I managed to lock my emotions away in a little steel box deep inside.

Telling my husband was the hardest thing I have ever done. We sat in the living room one evening, him on one sofa and me on the other, as we usually did when we came home from work. I stood up and walked over to turn the television off, lighting a cigarette as I sat down.

He looked at me disapprovingly, "I was watching that. And do you have to smoke in here?"

"I'm sorry," I replied, "I know you don't like it. I just need to talk to you, and this is not easy for me." I took a deep pull on the cigarette. "I want to leave... I don't love you anymore. We want different things out of life. You want to save for the future and I want to enjoy life – now. If I go you can find someone you love, you can have children, live the life you want. I just can't do it any more."

The look on his face was like a dagger in my guts. He had never knowingly hurt me, and look what I was doing. "But I love you," he stammered, "I don't understand. I don't mind if we don't have children. You know I don't."

"It isn't you, it's me," I rushed on. "I just want a different life. I'm sorry."

Over the next six weeks I tried to stay immune to the constant entreaties to stay, the offers to change. I went to see a pyschotherapist to see if I was crazy. I wavered on more than one occasion and found myself breaking down in the most peculiar places and at the strangest times, which was unlike me. However, I stuck to my guns and as the final week approached, I braced myself to go and break the news to my parents.

I was dreading telling them, and dreading letting them down. So far I had been the model, dutiful daughter and it was all about to change. What on earth was mother going to tell her hairdresser when she was asked how the children were? The more I thought about it the more I realized it was the, 'hairdresser syndrome' which had stopped me leaving a long time ago. Much nicer if your mother could say to the hairdresser, when asked about her family, "Lindsay's doing very well. She has a great job and a lovely husband." Now she was going to have to report, "Lindsay has left her job and her husband and is working on a beach somewhere. We think she's lost her mind." I wanted them to be proud of me and I was about to become a major disappointment.

I set off to see them, driving up the A1, the road stretching from London to Edinburgh. Straight for most of the way, all 410 miles of it. This road, which had been in existence since Roman times, had played a major part in my life. It had been an emotional road. Usually I was excited or happy when I was on it, going on holiday, or to see Steve before we were married. I remembered vividly driving up to my parents' house for my wedding, full of eager anticipation and joy. Now I was nervous, sad and apprehensive.

As I sped past the old coaching inns, I could almost see the ghosts of highwaymen galloping past me, faces hidden by black masks and their black capes streaming behind them. An ominous feeling grew and would not leave me, matched by the heavy rain as it fell on the windscreen.

My parents, both in their mid 60s, were retired but still active and busy. Mum had been a teacher and Dad a navigator in the Air Force, but now Mum was studying for a Master's degree at Cambridge University and Dad was studying Spanish at the Open University, and both were heavily involved in village life. The village was not far from Huntingdon, where they lived in a beautiful mock Tudor house. It was calm, peaceful and quintessentially English. I always enjoyed being there. They would have a lovely lunch ready – they were both excellent cooks – and Dad would open a new bottle of wine. After lunch, when the dishwasher was loaded, we would go into the lounge and the television would go on, and they would both fall asleep. *When should I tell them?* I wondered. *After lunch maybe, but I'm sure they'll realise something is wrong. Maybe I should just get it over with as soon as I get there.*

I had no idea what their reaction would be, and by the time I took the turn off the A1 for Huntingdon, my heart was pounding in my chest and my mouth was dry. I rehearsed my speech over and over again.

Twenty minutes later I swung into the gravel drive in front of my parents' house. The magnolia tree was blooming, as it had been eleven years before when I arrived for my wedding. I walked round to the back door and let myself in. Mum and Dad were in the kitchen, Dad wearing his chef's apron chopping onions expertly, and Mum washing up. I decided to get it over and done with, and when Dad poured me a pre-lunch sherry, we went into the lounge and sat down. I am sure they guessed. I took a deep breath.

"I guess you've realised I've come to see you for a reason." I sipped the sherry nervously. "Well, you're right, I've got something pretty big to tell you." The words tumbled out of my dry mouth in a rush, but only the basic, raw facts were there.

"My marriage is over. I've decided I want to leave my job so I'm going to the Maldives. I'm going to do my diving instructor's course and work as a diving instructor." I gulped the remainder of the sherry, its warmth spreading down my throat was comforting. There was total silence. Dad was staring at the sherry glass held between both hands in his lap, stunned. Then Mum said, "But what about your saucepans?"

"Sorry?" I asked, incredulously. Of every reaction I'd anticipated, this was not one of them. *What about my saucepans? What about my bloody saucepans?* My mouth dropped open. Had I heard correctly? I was leaving everything behind, making a life-changing move, and she was asking about the saucepans?

Mum and Dad had bought me a set of beautiful pans for my birthday and Christmas the previous year and yes, they were fabulous, and no, I was not taking them with me, and no, they were not in the storage facility. In fact they were the last thing on my mind. I had expected a whole range of questions, comments, disapproval and even tears, but I had not expected this.

"What are you going to do with your saucepans?" Mum persisted while Dad looked at me with sympathy and understanding in his eyes.

"I don't know Mum," I replied. "I'm leaving them in the house, just like everything else. The only things I'm taking are some clothes, my jewellery and my dive gear. The lock up just has my clothes in it."

"We'll help you however we can, love," said Dad, which was a great relief, but I could see the disappointment and concern on Mum's face.

Lunch was a subdued affair. I asked them if they would have power of attorney over my affairs and gave them the paperwork. They agreed, and although obviously sad, were more than prepared to help, which was a weight off my mind.

I left, saying goodbye to my parents, not knowing when I would be back. I was relieved to have told them and incredibly thankful they did not appear to be angry with me, but they were obviously concerned.

Driving back down the A1 to London, this time neither excited nor apprehensive, I was overwhelmed with sadness as the enormity of what I was about to do hit me. It was not a fun adventure any more, it was real, and people I cared about were being hurt and made miserable by what I was doing. I almost had second thoughts. Maybe it was the right thing to do and maybe it was wrong. I had no idea, but if I didn't try I would never know, and I might spend the next twenty years regretting it. I had to go. The ticket was booked and the flight was in two weeks, one way to Paradise – I hoped. And never mind about the bloody saucepans.

It was time to leave. I sank to the polished wooden floor in the hallway, looking at the front door and the vibrant colours of the stained glass, which I had always loved. "Okay Lindsay, come on, you can do it," I said to myself out loud. "All you have to do is walk through that door for the last time, post the keys through the letter box and get on a plane to your new life. Be brave woman." A lump came into my throat and my eyes filled with tears.

"I'm sorry George, sorry Henry," I whispered to my beloved Siamese cats as they rubbed themselves against me, trying to comfort me, not knowing I was about to betray them.

"Do it and stop being pathetic," I admonished myself. "This isn't helping anyone, you've made your decision now just go." I stood up and walked through the door without looking back, turned, locked it and heard the keys clatter on the hallway floor as I pushed them through the letter box. My husband would be home later to feed the cats.

"Goodbye old life," I murmured, through the tears trickling down my cheeks. They didn't stop until I boarded the plane, by which time I was sobbing uncontrollably. Once I was on the plane, wave after wave of relief, anticipation and happiness came over me. I had done it. I had bloody done it.

Within a few weeks I had qualified as a diving instructor, and started my first job teaching diving in Menorca where I enjoyed the work, although the dive school was in a shopping centre and the water was freezing. There were rocks instead of corals, and the odd cod instead of shoals of beautifully coloured fish. The job was for six months as the tourist season ended in October, when once again I was on the hunt for employment but dreaming of tropical beaches and warm water. I was determined to turn my dream into reality.

I already spoke French and German, and realised in Menorca that if I could speak Spanish too it would enhance my chances of getting work, especially in South America, definitely a place I wanted to go. By now I was forty-four, much older than your average diving instructor, but I decided to look at the PADI website for instructors' positions in tropical, Spanish speaking countries anyway, but did not put my age on the application. I looked a lot younger than my age, having short cropped, dyed blonde hair and was very fit and toned, due to years with a personal trainer in London, and the exercise of diving.

In less than a week I had a job offer. Neptuno, a German-run dive school in the town of Juan Dolio, south coast, Dominican Republic.

I was met at the airport by the owner of the dive school, Klaus. He showed a remarkable resemblance to Benny Hill. Short, rotund, red-haired and, as I was to find out, a temper to go with it. We drove to Juan Dolio, twenty-five minutes from the airport, and stopped at a bar opposite the dive school.

"This place is called Chocolate Bar," announced Klaus, in his heavy German accent. "And I can see my other instructors are here, so it's a perfect time to introduce you." We climbed out of the car and walked up to the wooden bar under a thatched palm roof.

"She is Marian and he is Uwe," said Klaus, pointing out a couple sat at the bar both wearing shorts and Neptuno dive sky blue T-shirts.

"Hi," I said a little nervously, as we walked up to them. Klaus had spoken in English, so I did the same, although not sure whether I should be speaking German.

"Hallo," replied Marian, smiling warmly at me flicking back her long blonde hair behind her shoulders. Uwe raised his glass and grinned, nodding his head in welcome. They both looked to be my age, which was a relief, and Uwe looked even older, due to his lack of hair and weatherbeaten face. Klaus bought me my first *cuba libre* (rum and coke), and afterwards took me over the road to see the dive school. As soon as I got there I felt a rush of happiness, and a big grin spread over my face. It was exactly what I had been looking for. The dive school was built of wood with a palm leaf roof and situated on a white sandy beach, in front of the glistening Caribbean Sea. Although it was six in the evening, it was toasty warm.

The next day I was free, to get over the jet lag, and set off to explore Juan Dolio. It was a pleasant, bustling little seaside town, consisting of a road along the beach three miles in length and not a lot else. On the beach side of the street were seven or eight hotels, and on the other side gift shops, restaurants and bars. Tourists of all nationalities wandered along the road in swimwear and flip-flops, and motorbike taxis known as *motoconchos* buzzed up and down. I had decided to walk to the dive school, but it was very hot, and a *motoconcho* stopped.

"Taxi?" asked the driver, flashing his beautiful white teeth.

"Err, I don't think so," I replied, terrified of being on the back of a motorbike. Steve always wanted one and I'd said no, as I thought they were too dangerous

"Taxi?" he asked again.

Oh sod it, I thought. *I might as well give it a go.* I spoke no Spanish, but luckily he was Haitian so we chatted in French. He explained how to climb on, and off we went with me hanging onto him for dear life. Over the next few trips I became used to them, learnt how to climb on and off without burning my leg on the exhaust pipe, and eventually, although it took a while, how to sit on the back of the bike without holding onto anything. And dead proud of myself I was too. The *motoconcho* driver was called Liko and he became my personal chauffeur, taking me to work every day and picking me up from Chocolate Bar after work.

The job was fine. There were two dives in the morning and the afternoons were spent in the pool doing training exercises. The dive school was well run, as you would expect from a German operation, but there was a degree of being shouted at by Klaus. We were not allowed to leave in the evening until he said so, and a missing piece of equipment could cause us to wait until seven o'clock before we were allowed home. I often had to fight to keep my mouth shut and forget I used to be a company director.

In the afternoons, we would encourage the guests from the various hotels to try out diving in the hotel pools and try and sign them up for a diving course. As I spoke French, German and English, and given my sales and marketing background, it was not difficult for me to increase the sales so, within a few weeks, I was put in charge of my own hotel, Talanquera, and had my own little hut on the beach. This meant I was diving a lot less, but I was shouted at less too, as I was out of range of the Germans.

I was not alone in my hut, as apart from the rats, I had my very own staff. Jason, Billy, Frank and Martin. Jason was Haitian, in the country legally, and in charge of water sports, which involved handing out free masks and snorkels, fins and kayaks. The other three were Dominican and walked along the beach and by the pool, signing tourists up for pool dives, where I could then sell them a diving package.

These four were the envy of their friends as they could spend all day long talking to foreign tourists. Sitting at my little plastic table in front of the hut, I asked Martin one day, "Why do you want to do this job?"

"It helps my English," he replied and paused before saying, "and maybe one day I will meet a nice foreign girl."

"What's wrong with Dominican girls?" I asked curiously.

"Nothing, but there are only two ways we can make something of our lives here," he answered. "One is to leave the country and go somewhere with better opportunities to work and earn more money, and the other is to marry someone who has money, who can help us here."

"Well, why don't you just leave then," I asked. He burst out laughing. "We can't. We need a visa and they are almost impossible to get unless you are married to someone from that country."

"Ah, sorry, I had no idea," I apologised. The guys who worked for me earned the basic wage of £100 a month, 5000 Dominican pesos, and although they wanted a foreign girlfriend they were not 'sanky pankies'.

A 'sanky panky' is a Dominican or Haitian man who goes out with a foreign woman with one aim, to extort as much money from her as possible. Love does not enter the equation. They are con men pure and simple and will normally prey on older and larger ladies, who might find it hard to find love in their own country. The 'sankies' are excellent at their jobs, and having wooed the ladies for a while, and feeling the fish on the hook, begin their plans to extort money by appealing to the better natures of their victims. They always used the same lines, which had been successful with others in the past. It would start off with fairly small amounts.

"I would love to keep in touch with you when you go, but I need a mobile phone."

"My trainers have fallen apart and I have no other shoes."

Before the woman would leave to return home they would usually try and extort a larger amount. "My mother is dying of cancer and if I cannot find money for her operation she will die. Please help me to save my mother's life?" The requests for money do not end once the ensnared victim has landed back in her home country.

"I'm in jail and need you to send me some money so I can be released."

"I've lost my job and haven't eaten in days."

The cash would be sent via Western Union and there would be a constant queue of sankies waiting for money. The expert sankies had several women on the go at the same time, and there were often complications when two would return to see them at the same time.

The sankified ladies would come to my hut to chat about how in love they were, and how this guy was so different. I was warned to keep my mouth shut and not to tell the women the true nature of their beloved, and as I had to live there I obliged. To be honest, I doubt many of the women would have believed me anyway.

Jason always wanted a foreign girlfriend, but he was very short, so he had no success. He had been working for me for about a year, and in the country for two years, when one day a visitor turned up for him. It was his ex-girlfriend from Haiti who he had not seen since he left, two years before. She was seven months pregnant and said the baby was his.

I sat Jason down and said to him gently, "Listen Jason, there is no way this is your baby. She can't have been pregnant for over two years!"

"Lindsay," he replied patiently, "you clever, but you not unnerstan' my country, Haiti. We have Tropical Syndrome. The woman become pregnant, but if her man go away, the baby not grows as she sad an' missin' her man. She can be pregnant for years, 'til she know she see her man again, and she happy and the baby begins to grows again."

So now you know. The baby was born two months later. Jason had originally left Haiti when he saw his girlfriend kissing his best friend, and he was angry with both of them. He explained to me that God had punished him for being angry by making the baby look exactly like his best friend.

Jason was intelligent. He could speak fluent English, French, Creole and Spanish, but it was impossible for me to change his way of thinking. Dominicans and Haitians had entrenched beliefs, which I could not question or change. These beliefs had been passed down from parents to children through generations, and in their eyes were true.

As the dive school flourished, new instructors arrived including Fred the longhaired French hippy and Neil, taking time out from his IT work in England, and my social life took off. We worked hard, but played hard too. Every night we would be out at a local bar where there was live music.

There was music everywhere in the country. In the bars, in the street, in the houses, in the shops. Dominicans love dancing and you would see people dancing in the supermarkets. I was always being asked to dance and unlike the UK, the women do not dance together around their handbags, instead the men come and ask you to dance. Very gentlemanly and, not for the first time, I felt as if I were back in the UK of the 1940s or 1950s.

Apart from the tourists who came and went, Juan Dolio was like a village and I soon got to know people so everywhere I went would be greeted not just with a, "*Hola!*" but a handshake, and sometimes a hug and a kiss. In no time I felt I belonged.

I found myself smiling all the time. Whenever I caught the *guagua* (bus) everyone would greet me when I clambered on, and I greeted them back. The *guagua* picks you up on the road wherever you are, and lets you off wherever you want to get off. There is no need for bus stops. The person next to you always chats, and men offer you their seat. Of course there is always music on the bus, and people singing along. Looking out of the windows there were things to smile at; cars falling apart, six people on a motorbike, cows, goats or chickens wandering in the road.

I was enjoying myself. I loved my job, and what I loved most was the optimism. I was used to a life of pessimism and moaning. Moaning about the weather, taxes, house prices, work, or transport. Here everyone seemed to look on the bright side, which was refreshing. I would watch the tourists climbing onto the coach to take them back to the airport at the end of their holidays, and I felt blessed I did not have to leave.

I was originally thinking of leaving the DR after my six-month contract was up, but after I had been there for a few months I was already thinking about staying longer. And the longer I stayed, the more people I got to know and the happier I became. I was not looking for a relationship, but I was leading a fun and carefree life and very happy with it. I had at last found what I was looking for. Sun, sand, sea, diving and laughter.

And freedom.

THE DOMINICAN REPUBLIC IS SITUATED IN THE NORTHERN PART OF the Caribbean and is part of Hispaniola, an island discovered by Christopher Columbus in 1492 and used as his springboard for the Spanish conquest of the Caribbean. The DR takes up roughly two thirds of the island with the western third being Haiti. The area of the country is 48,730 km² – twice the size of Wales – making it the second largest country in the Caribbean after Cuba. The northern coast lies on the Atlantic Ocean and the south on the Caribbean. The capital, Santo Domingo, is situated in the middle of the southern coast. To the north is the United States, to the east Puerto Rico, west Cuba and south is the Caribbean Sea all the way to the coast of Venezuela.

The Dominican Republic is not a typical tropical Caribbean island. Its size means it consists of more than beaches, although there are over 1600 kilometres of coastline. The interior of the country is diverse with mountain ranges, fertile plains, deserts, and rain forests. The highest mountain range in the Dominican Republic - indeed, in the Caribbean - is the Cordillera Central with the four highest peaks in the Caribbean region. The highest is Pico Duarte (3,098 metres / 10,164 feet). The centre of the country has fertile valleys, especially the Cibao region, which are the hub of the country's agriculture, in particular rice, bananas, coffee and cocoa.

Although Hispaniola is one island, the two countries, the Dominican Republic and Haiti, are completely different in terms of culture, language and people. As they developed, the country we know as Haiti, having been colonised by the French, concentrated on growing sugar cane, becoming one of the most productive colonies in the northern hemisphere. In order to achieve these massive levels of sugar production, the French imported huge numbers of African slaves. By 1790 there were more than half a million black slaves and only 30,000 whites, and 27,000 freemen who were black and mulatto (mixed race).

However, in the Dominican Republic it was a different story. The population was less than Haiti and subsistence farming the main occupation. As the Spanish weren't interested in sugar production, they didn't import large numbers of slaves. By 1790 there were 125,000 white Spanish landowners, 60,000 slaves and 25,000 black and mulatto freemen. The blacks were a minority and as the Spanish were encouraged to marry both the freemen and the black slaves, the mulatto population grew.

Although many Dominicans today like to say they are descended directly from the Indians, the majority are a mix of the African and Spanish, with 85% of the population being brown skinned or mulatto, and the rest of pure Spanish or pure African descent. The proximity to Haiti, one of the poorest nations in the world, brings with it particular issues for the Dominican Republic. The population of the DR is estimated at 10 million but of these it is impossible to determine how many are Haitian who have entered the country both legally and illegally. Estimates on the number of Haitians in the country range from one to two million. Whilst many Haitians work, especially in construction projects, up to 20% of the country have a different nationality, culture and speak a different language, which brings with it special problems for the DR, specifically in the areas of health care and education. The Dominican Republic is a former Spanish colony and the official language is Spanish. The official language of Haiti is Creole, which has its roots in French.

CHAPTER TWO
THE MAN FROM BARAHONA

ONE EVENING I WAS OUT WITH NEIL AND FRED, TWO OF THE DIVE instructors, in Chocolate Bar in Juan Dolio. The bar was full as usual, music blaring out and I wandered through the crowd talking to students I had been diving with that morning, sometimes stopping to dance with Dominicans, but I knew I shouldn't stay up too late as I was diving in the morning, so decided to leave.

"Neil, Fred I'm off now," I shouted above the din. "See you at work in the morning!"

"Wake me up please," Fred shouted back and I grinned and began to walk out of the bar to hail a *motoconcho*. Behind me I heard someone speak, trying to catch my attention, "I Danilo. I take you home on *pasola* (scooter)?"

I turned around. In front of me stood a Dominican man. He was not overly tall, the colour of Cadbury's milk chocolate with very short, dark hair. He was wearing a tight, sleeveless T-shirt, which showed off a fabulous body, very muscular and well defined, without an ounce of fat. As I looked up at his face he smiled, and he had the most dazzling smile, with a little gap in his front teeth. He was gorgeous.

"Yes, I would love a lift home. Thank you Danilo." What harm would it do? I climbed onto the back of his yellow *pasola*, put my arms around his waist and off we went on the ten-minute ride back to my house.

"*Gracias*," I said, as we pulled up at the front of my apartment building.

"You are welcome," he replied smiling. "Tomorrow I come for you." I laughed. "I am working tomorrow, I don't get home till six."

"Tomorrow I come for you at six o'clock," he said determinedly, his eyes fixed on mine.

The following evening I arrived back at my apartment, tired, dishevelled and crusted with salt after a day's diving. There stood Danilo together with a policeman.

"Hello, how are you? I wait for you." Danilo announced, with his amazing white smile. I was to discover Dominican men do not like going anywhere alone, they have at least one friend with them and even when courting have a chaperone.

"Listen guys, I need to eat, I've been diving all day and I'm starving. Do you mind if I eat my dinner?" I asked, wearily.

"We need eat too," replied Danilo disarmingly, smiling again.

"Fine, come on upstairs to the apartment then," I replied. "It's prawn curry tonight, is that okay for you?"

Danilo looked at the policeman quizzically, "*Que es* 'prawn'? *Que es* 'curry'?" I had no idea how to say prawn in Spanish and once inside the apartment, I showed them.

"Oh... *camarones!*" he exclaimed. I had no idea neither of them had ever eaten prawns, as they were expensive, and I had no idea neither of them had eaten anything spicy. They were so looking forward to trying the prawns, but both sat there sweating and giving each other pleading glances, murmuring '*picante*' at each other, which means spicy or hot. From then on the policeman was always known as *Picante*.

We met most evenings for the next couple of weeks, slowly learning about each other. Danilo told me he had been brought up in the mountains above Barahona, a town in the south west of the country.

"What about your parents?" I asked.

"They both dead now. My father, he left my mother when I four years old and took me and my brother Biembo to live in *La Loma*."

"*La Loma?*" I asked.

"It is the mountain above Barahona. We went on donkey, it take very many time and is cold."

"But what about food, were there shops? And where did you live?" I persisted.

"My father, he build little house of wood, with zinc roof. We sleep on banana leaf inside rice sack, or the rats they eat skin on our feets. We cook on fire outside, is called *fogon*, and we eat what we grow – banana and yuca. Sometime we kill chicken."

"And what about school?" I asked, incredulous at the idea of living like this.

"My father, he teach me read and write, and when I fourteen I walk down mountain to school on Monday, come back Friday. I wear shoes round neck so they not dirty. It take four hours to walk. I no like school, as I older than other children. Better to be in mountain. Is it matter I no go to school many time?"

"No, I suppose not. It's just a shame for you," I said.

"Now I want very much to learn many things," he said smiling at me. "You teach me."

Danilo didn't seem to want to know anything about me. He knew I was English and that was enough. Things which are considered important to a relationship in England didn't seem to concern him at all. We didn't dance around each other assessing our respective suitability as partners. I didn't have to ask my friends what they thought of him, be concerned about him meeting my family, working out his career potential. He had no idea how old I was – he didn't ask – he had no idea what I had done with my life before I came to the Dominican Republic. None of that mattered. He was interested in me as I was now. And slowly I realised I was looking forward to seeing him every night, and when I was with him I loved every minute.

One evening I was curled up on the sofa in my apartment, chatting with Fred, the French instructor who lived in the apartment downstairs, when the door opened and in strode three Dominican men. One had a Bobby Shaftoe-type large bundle in a sheet over his shoulder. They said nothing, walked past us into the bedroom, reappeared with only the sheet, and left.

I looked at Fred, "What the hell was that?" He gave a Gallic shrug and we walked into the bedroom to check it out. There was a pile of clothes and books covering the bed and some of the clothes looked suspiciously like Danilo's.

"I think he just moved in," I muttered. I wasn't overly concerned, but things appeared to be moving very fast. I thought this was something you discussed after you had been together for months, not a couple of weeks. And a few days later, while we were relaxing and I was involved in a new book, he said to me, "I need tell you some things."

"What things?" I asked distractedly, as I carried on reading.

"I have childrens," he said nervously. "Is it problem for you I have childrens?"

"No, I assumed you would have some somewhere. Most men of your age do," I answered, putting the book down slowly. "So, tell me about your children."

"They are boys. They live with me," he answered, seeming a little relieved.

"Er... I thought you lived here, so where are the children and, more importantly, where is their mother? And how many children?" I could feel myself starting to get anxious about what was coming next.

"They have no mothers. Mothers gone, they no want my childrens. They are boys, come I take you see my boys." He stood up decisively and, pulling me by the hand, dragged me downstairs to the car park.

I clambered onto the back of the *pasola* and off we went to Danilo's house, only five minutes away. We turned off the main beach road onto a dusty potholed track and after a minute or so riding through the woods, arrived at a two-storey apartment block with a pool and in the corner of the garden was his house. The little house had brick walls and a zinc-sheeted roof. There was a tiny kitchen, toilet, two small bedrooms and a couple of Dominican women slouched on the couch in a tiny living area. Danilo nodded at them and led me through into one of the bedrooms.

"My boys here," he whispered. The three boys, Dany eleven, Alberto nine and Christian six, were all asleep in a single bed. Dany and Alberto at one end, Christian at the other.

"But Danilo they are so cute," I exclaimed, with a big smile on my face.

"They are my childrens," Danilo announced proudly.

"But where is their mother?" I asked.

"The mother of Dany and Alberto she leave them when Alberto three week old. She has another man. Then they live with my mother in capital, but my mother she die, so they live with me."

"So... where did you live in the capital. I thought you lived in Barahona?"

"I move to capital when I eighteen. My father, he sell cow for clothes and passage. I go be a policeman, but not easy to be policeman, so in day I work construction and at night I security man. I no have house. Childrens with me in cardboard box. Big box. Then I have other wife and we have Christian, and we move here Juan Dolio. But she go with other man to Spain so I and boys alone again." I was appalled at the life the children had had, it seemed incredible and I looked down fondly at them for a minute or two before we left.

We lived together, just the two of us, for only a week – I couldn't stop thinking about the boys. It seemed wrong they were in another house, although they were being looked after by other people.

I decided a few things needed clearing up between us, so one morning before I left for work, I sat at the dining room table drinking my coffee and having a cigarette, and casually asked, "Danilo, you've mentioned two wives. Were there any more? Are you divorced?" I looked up at him, as he wiped down the kitchen counter.

"They my only wives. I have no more. I am serious man, *hombre serio* we say in Espany. And when I say wife, I mean Dominican wife. Many people here no marry in church or with judge, it cost many money. You live in same house, you are wife. You my wife now."

I nearly choked on my coffee and as I banged the mug down too hard on the wooden table, some slopped out of the side.

"I am your wife?" I asked incredulously, getting up to grab a cloth to wipe the table.

"Yes, you is my wife, it is good no?" he asked, putting his arm around my waist.

"Yes... fine I suppose. Anyway, so if there are no other wives I think your boys should move in here with us. It's not right them living there and you here, and you have to go running back and forwards all day to see them and feed them and look after them. Bring them here to live, they can have the spare room, and at least it has a double bed, there will be plenty of room for them." He looked at me, surprised.

"Are you sure you want my childrens here? Will you hit them?" I was stunned.

"Of course not!" I replied, shocked. "What on earth makes you say that?"

"Because it hatping before, with number two wife, Diomaris. She like her child Christian more than Dany and Alberto, so she hit them sometime. Sometime she hit them hard. I no want person hit them hard."

"Well, I don't hit children," I said, "so bring them to live here."

The following day Danilo arrived home on the *pasola* with the three boys perched behind him. Dressed identically in yellow T-shirts and blue shorts, with Spiderman knapsacks on their backs, stuffed with all their worldly goods, and toothbrushes in hand, they came cautiously into the apartment. Danilo directed them into the spare bedroom where their little eyes opened wide at the double bed. They opened wider at the sight of the fridge and the television. They had no toys, very few clothes and were terrified. I am not sure if they were overwhelmed in moving away from their house, where they knew everyone and everything, or whether they were scared I would treat them as Diomaris had.

"Danilo," I whispered. "Why don't they speak? Why are they just sitting there on the sofa?"

"They know not speak till I say. They not speak when I working, they must be quiet. They behave good. They be fine soon, you see."

I walked over to the children, "Do you want to watch television?" Three little faces looked up at me. They looked at each other and Alberto whispered, "*Si*." I turned the television onto one of the children's programmes and they sat there staring at it.

After a few minutes Dany piped up, "Is water to drink?"

"Of course," I said smiling, and led him over to the fridge. "Here is water, Coca Cola, juice. If you want something just take it. The glasses are in the cupboard up here." He stood staring at me blankly, so I poured him some water and was about to do the same for Alberto and Christian, but Alberto came over and pointed to the Coca Cola. I poured him a glass and one for Christian and they scuttled back to the sofa, watching me warily as I began to cook dinner.

And so began family life. Danilo would get up with me and take me to work on the *pasola*, and come back and take the kids to school. When he met me, he was working for an insurance company in the capital. He had gone to college on his day off whilst working in construction, and eventually landed an office job. The company had holiday apartments in Juan Dolio, which is why he and his family had moved here. As well as working in the office, he was made caretaker of the apartments, a much better place for the children to be brought up.

However, he was made redundant from his job in the capital just before we met and bought a bigger *pasola* with his redundancy money, as it was our only means of transport. He would clean our apartment and go to the apartment building where he was still the caretaker, sort out any issues, and feed his dog, Can Can the pit bull. The first time I met her I was terrified. I had never seen a pit bull up close before, I just knew they killed people and their owners were usually skinheads with tattoos and piercings. Eventually I plucked up the courage to pat her and Can Can was startled, Dominicans do not pat dogs, they are used for protection, not treated as members of the family.

I was surprised how Danilo would happily do the cleaning and organise the house. He paid bills, he did the shopping, all I had to do was go to work. I had never met a man who would do so much for me. But at the same time I was wary, as I was concerned he wanted money like the sankies, so I would leave money in the house, but he never took a penny.

Once he had picked me up from work he cooked dinner, which was always something Dominican, such as mashed plantains with a tin of sardines on top. Or stewed chicken, and rice and beans. He would put it all on a plate and give it to me to eat. I would eat as much as I wanted, (usually not much, unsurprisingly) then it would be passed to the boys to eat, one at a time, and finally he would eat what was left. As I was not enamoured with this food, I would sometimes cook, and each of us would have our own plate. The kids had never seen this before, everyone having their own plate of food. I also instigated always eating with a spoon and not with their hands. No one would start eating until everyone had their food or leave the table until everyone had finished, and dinner was a time for us all to talk together. This last one was very strange for them as they had been brought up not to talk at dinner – Danilo had told them the rice would come down their noses if they spoke while eating.

I would cook basic food such as spaghetti bolognese and chilli con carne without too much chilli. I had learnt spicy food was a no-no. But even this was strange for the kids, and, more often than not, they would distract me by telling me to look at something out of the window, and throw the food into a plant pot. They felt the same way about my cooking as I felt about Danilo's, but eventually we all became accustomed to each other's food. We all adapted, I would use less hot spices and Danilo would use less oil and salt.

Although edible, I was not keen on Dominican food. Unlike much of the food in the Caribbean, it is not spicy and lacks flavour. The main meal is eaten at noon, with everyone laying down tools at exactly twelve o'clock to eat. It is almost always the same. Rice, beans stewed in a sauce, and a small amount of meat, either chicken or beef, again in a sauce. It is high in salt and oil. There is usually a small salad on the side and always slices of avocado when they are in season. As well as the ubiquitous rice and beans, Dominicans eat plantains with either fried salami, or sardines, and sometimes whole fish, often snapper (*chillo*). Stewed goat is eaten on special occasions, and this is always served a little spicy. Sometimes you can eat pork chops, and there are fried chicken shops – the local equivalent of fast food. The fried chicken is sold together with *tostones*, fried plantain chips.

Cooking rice is an art. As well as rice and water, plenty of salt and oil are added. Once the water has been absorbed, a plastic bag is placed firmly over the rice. I suggested using a lid but this was pooh-poohed and it was explained it has to be a plastic bag. The rice is cooked until it burns, and everyone fights over the burnt bits known as *con con*. It took me years to get it right.

The other major issue for us was the language barrier. My Spanish was very limited, and although Danilo spoke a little English, the kids spoke none. One night I said to them in my broken Spanish, "Do you want pasta or rice to eat?" Three little faces looked blankly at me.

"Pasta?" queried Dany.

"Yes, pasta," I said. "You know, *espaghetti*."

"Oh, *espaghetti*!" they laughed, and Alberto went into the bathroom and came out holding a tube of toothpaste.

"*Eso es pasta*," he announced. The word for toothpaste was *pasta de dientes*, shortened to *pasta*. No wonder they were confused.

I was slowly picking up Spanish but the Dominican dialect misses out the letters from words, and often the word is not completely pronounced either. If I wanted to know what a word meant and looked it up in a dictionary, it was impossible. For example, Danilo would ask me,

"*Dondé tu ta?*" and I knew this meant where are you, but I could not find the word '*ta*' in the dictionary. It was actually, *dondé tu estas*. And this was the same with so many words – *autopista* was the word for motorway and they would say, *pita*.

Danilo would often speak English, although as my Spanish improved the English took a back seat. One day he phoned me at work and yelled down the phone, "I lose my teeth!"

"Where are your teeth?" I asked incredulously, thinking I must have misheard him.

"I need your teeth. I come now for take your teeth." He arrived at the beach a few minutes later, announcing I should give him my teeth. It turned out he meant keys. There were several instances like this, which added plenty of humour to life.

It was astonishing how far apart our worlds were. Danilo had no idea about DIY. He could hardly change a plug as he had been brought up without electricity. He'd never used a fridge, coffee machine, liquidiser, or a can opener. Even after I showed him how to use one he would still open cans with a knife. We would watch the Discovery channel. He refused to believe heart transplants happen, and insisted the world was flat, as if it was round we would fall off. He was also religious and believed everything the Bible said. I explained we came from monkeys, which he vehemently denied.

"If we came from monkeys, then why there still monkeys? Did some monkeys say they not want be a human?" No answer to that. He was always asking questions.

"Does the water in the sea come from rivers?"

"Yes," I would reply."

"But river water is not salty?"

"No."

"So, where does the salt come from in the sea?" And, "Where does the rain come from?"

"Clouds. The water evaporates from the sea and makes clouds."

"Why is rain not salty then?"

Apart from the practical side of things, the cultural gap was enormous. My first few months in the Dominican Republic, I saw it through the eyes of a tourist. I only went onto the main road, to the bars, restaurants and shops. I went into the local town, San Pedro de Macoris, once a fortnight to the main supermarket. But while I was teaching Danilo about geography, history, science, he was teaching me too, about living in poverty, about natural medical cures, about the importance of family and looking after each other. Very different from the priorities I'd grown up with, which stressed the importance of your job, the house you lived in and the car you drove. He would take me to see his friends, and whilst they only lived a few minutes from the main street, it was an area no tourists, and indeed most expatriates, didn't see.

I had no idea over half of the country lived in such appalling poverty. In the towns the houses were made of breezeblocks or wood, usually with zinc sheeting on the roof. The design was always the same with a little outside terrace for sitting on, and inside, through the door, a living area, behind which was a small kitchen. There would be a curtain hanging over a gap in the wall in the living area leading to the bedroom. Some houses had more than one bedroom, and some had bathrooms, but not all. Most houses had bars on the windows and doors. Bottled gas was used for cooking by those who could afford it, and those who couldn't cooked outside on a charcoal fire.

In the forest area behind the main street in Juan Dolio the houses were all made of wood, and were known as *casitas* – literally a little house – where we would visit people Danilo knew. Everyone was very welcoming and would pull up a plastic chair for me and we'd all sit outside in front of a group of huts. We'd chat and watch the goings on, surrounded as we were by children running around naked, chickens pecking at the ground and there were always a few street dogs lying in the shade. Often someone would be bathing in a large tub and there would be a large pot of something bubbling away on the open fire. However poor these people were, they would always share food or drink with you, even when it meant going without themselves.

The homes inside were basic, usually one room with the zinc roof weighted down with rocks to stop it blowing off in the wind. There was no running water or electricity and everyone used a public latrine shared with twenty or so houses. The room had a bare earth floor and would be furnished with a bed, plastic chairs, sometimes a table (always with a cloth) and a picture of Jesus or the Virgin Mary on the wall. Despite the poverty every *casista* would have a television.

There were hundreds of homes like this, built up in little shanty villages, lived in by Dominicans and Haitians. It made me feel very humble.

For those who worked, the average wage was 5000 pesos a month, around £100. Out of this there was rent to pay, even for a little wooden shack, and for a small house it would be 1000 pesos. It did not leave much for anything else.

This level of poverty affected all elements of life. It became obvious that emotionally, people in the DR reacted differently to things than I did, having been raised in the UK. I could only think that every effort went into survival, rather than nurturing and loving their children as they were growing up. Danilo's children had never had a bedtime story read to them, they had never been cuddled, never had help with homework. It was the same for everyone who came from a similar background – approximately 40% of the population lived in extreme poverty, and another 40% were not much better off. As my Spanish improved I tried to have conversations with Danilo about this.

"Danilo, why do you love me?"

"Because you love me," he replied.

"Well, what do you think love is?" I persisted.

"It jus' is," was his reply.

"When I'm not with you I miss you," I told him. It was true, I did. For some reason I was like a sixteen-year-old with her first boyfriend. I missed him when we were apart, which was ridiculous, a feeling I had not had for years.

"I miss you too," he replied with a huge smile.

It was impossible to have a deep, meaningful conversation, and in the end I gave up trying and told myself it was not important. People lived for the day. As long as there was enough food to eat, they were happy. And everywhere we went people did appear to be happy.

This lack of emotional maturity meant many Dominicans would exhibit childlike behaviour, something constantly commented on by those expatriates who had lived here for a while. It was this childlike behaviour, which gave Dominicans their charm. There was, however, a blurred line between truth and lies. Just as a child would not tell the truth if they felt they would get into trouble, nor would the Dominicans I met. They would tell you what they thought you wanted to hear, as they were desperate to please. If you asked directions from a stranger and they did not know, they would send you in the wrong direction rather than saying they didn't know. If you asked if it would be sunny tomorrow they would say yes rather than disappoint you.

Danilo's children were very well behaved on the whole. They would do anything their father asked them to, such as clean the house or wash the dishes. They would never dream of arguing or answering back to either him or me. Dany was a bit jealous of me at first, but he managed to get over that after a couple of years. Alberto had a very sunny and helpful disposition and would always help me with the cooking. Christian hardly spoke at all though, and I thought it was possible he had some sort of mental retardation. When it was just he and I together he was very chatty.

Unfortunately, one evening, Danilo and I were dancing in Guila Café, a local bar with a live band every Monday night, where we would regularly go. He and I were dancing together when suddenly a man tapped me on the shoulder, wanting to dance with me. I was confused till I realised his female partner wanted to dance with Danilo. I saw the look on Danilo's face. Pure fury. After the dance he came back, sat down with me, and muttered gruffly "Later", so I knew not to ask. We got back to the apartment and he sat me down on the couch.

"That woman is Diomaris," he said through gritted teeth. "She left me and boys as she not happy with us, and she went with Spanish man to live in Spain. In three years I hear nothing. Now she back and she want see Christian."

"I can't see any problem in that – she's his mother," I replied, not knowing there were plenty of problems to come. She would meet Christian after school, shower him with presents until one day she arrived at our apartment yelling like a banshee, dragging Christian behind her.

"You never see him again! Ever! I his mother, not that bitch," she screamed, pointing at me, and she started clawing at Danilo's face in a white rage. She ran past him to try and get to me. I was sitting on the sofa with the other boys, my mouth open. I had never seen anything like this crazy screaming woman before, and the boys cowered behind me, shaking in terror. Danilo managed to grab her and pushed her outside and she went, still screaming and taking Christian with her.

She took him to Bani, about two hours away, to her parents, under strict instruction I was not allowed to see him.

After much toing and froing, Danilo agreed to sign the paperwork to allow her to take Christian to Spain and he left for a new life there with her and her Spanish husband. There was nothing either of us could do about it, and we knew he would have more opportunities and better schooling in Spain, so we accepted the situation. Dany and Alberto did not seem too upset about their younger brother leaving, although Danilo and I missed him dreadfully at first.

Dany and Alberto, like their father, always wanted to help me and do things to make me happy. They were never happier than when I would take them to the shops so they could help with the shopping, or when I read them a bedtime story. I introduced them to *Winnie the Pooh*, and tried to tell them English fairy stories in my basic Spanish. I tried to teach them some English, and we covered the apartment with Post-It notes with the words for things in Spanish and English so we could all learn. I was beginning to enjoy being a mother for the first time.

Dominican culture continued to dominate and frustrate my life. If I shopped for a week and filled the fridge, everything would be gone within hours. It was not that the kids ate it all – they simply gave it away. Dominicans will share everything, and I would find not only were they 'sharing' food, they also shared sheets, towels and whatever else they could get their hands on. It was usually Alberto who did this and in my mind it was stealing, but to him it was normal to help out his friends as he always had, and he saw everything in the house as belonging to all of us. I would see *motoconcho* drivers wearing my T-shirts, and it was frustrating when things disappeared all the time. I spotted a little Haitian lad wearing my Timberland boots one day on his way to school and as soon as I got home I yelled at Alberto, "Why the hell did you give my boots to that kid?"

"It wasn't me," he replied shakily.

"I know it was you, will you just tell me why?" I demanded.

"Because he didn't have any shoes, and you don't wear them a lot and he wanted to go to school."

What was I supposed to do? They could not comprehend when I said something belonged to me, and I wanted no one else to take it, use it or eat it. The concept of personal ownership did not exist.

You could only buy limited groceries in Juan Dolio. I would come home from a days diving, looking forward to drinking a Coca Cola and the bottle I had bought the day before at the supermarket in San Pedro would be gone.

"Where is my bloody Coca Cola?" I would scream. "Alberto, have you drunk it?"

"No fui yo," he would answer – "It wasn't me."

"Yo no se," Dany would pipe up – "I don't know."

These phrases became the bane of my life and although pretty calm over most things, the disappearing food and other items would send me crazy. I would rant and rave every time I went to the fridge to look for something and it had disappeared. I had no idea if this was something all children did, regardless of nationality, or just a Dominican thing.

Neither would they be tidy and organised. I never knew a cutlery drawer could cause such stress. I would put the knives in one section, the forks in another and the spoons in another. The boys and Danilo would just open it and throw everything in. Every day I would reorganise it and by the next it was in the same state.

In the end I started throwing things in too, as the boys proved impossible to train, and it stressed me less if I accepted it and did it their way. Does it matter if the forks are not in the fork place and the knives in the knife place? Learning that lesson took a long time. If you could accept the way Dominicans did things, life was less stressful. You had to decide what was important and what was not. A messy cutlery drawer was not important in the scheme of things.

I also discovered a Dominican trait was to do things the easy way, or not finish a job properly. When it was Alberto's turn to wash the dishes he displayed this to perfection. If something were difficult to wash he would not bother with it but instead hide it, or throw it away. We were always finding dirty pots and pans in the oven, the fridge or freezer, or stuck in the back of a cupboard. Once a week I had to go and check the dustbins and pull out dirty pans. Thank goodness I had not brought my nice saucepans with me.

But apart from the frustrations I had, we laughed from morning to night. We took the children to the zoo, going on the *guagua* into the capital, and we would go to the beach on Sunday and stuff our faces with *pulpo*, octopus mixed with tomatoes and onions, lime juice and a little vinegar. Danilo would rent a pedalo and he and I would pedal and the kids dive off into the water. Danilo and I would go out at night on the *pasola* with no protective clothing and no helmets. I remember thinking I had never been so happy as we rode along the beach road with the warm night air blowing through my hair. I had found the joy I was looking for.

We would meet up with his friends, like Saya, a pot bellied Dominican who always seemed to be around, and Fred and Ian, the dive instructors. Everyone seemed to know Danilo, wherever we went there were people to talk to or laugh with. Most nights we were out dancing at different bars, or eating with friends in restaurants, although I would try and get back at a reasonable hour when I was working the next day.

He wanted to show me Barahona, his hometown, so we rented an SUV, known as a *jipeta* here, and off we went for the weekend. Danilo sitting next to me in the front and the kids in the back. It was a long drive, over four hours, all along the southern coast of the country going west, and my first time driving in the country as Danilo couldn't drive. We went through the capital where the driving is the craziest I have ever seen, especially with Danilo navigating yelling, "Turn left" when I was in the right hand lane and screaming, "Go" even though the traffic lights were on red.

We drove through the towns of San Cristobal and Bani, and eventually the landscape changed into desert, with cacti growing at the side of the road and there were fewer and fewer vehicles. Slowly the mountains came into view, rising majestically above the blue Caribbean ocean and on the right were sugar cane fields as far as the eye could see. As we moved closer I could see Haitian men, stripped to the waist with the sweat glistening on their muscular bodies as they chopped the cane, the same way it had been done for centuries. The hump-backed oxen stood in the shade of the trees swatting the myriads of flies from their backs with their raggedy tails. It was like another world, and I was fascinated by it.

We stayed in a hotel in the centre of town, the kids in one room and us next door and we went to the local *pica pollo* (fried chicken) shop in town for dinner. The next day Danilo's brother, Cristian, came with us and we drove around the whole area. He was not Danilo's blood brother, but Danilo had stayed with Cristian's family while he went to school in Barahona. We drove along the coast road, stopping at places where the rivers running down from the mountains met the ocean, bathing in cold river water, whilst looking at the sea and feasting on fresh fish and frosty *Presidente* beer.

We drove inland to see the amazing Lake Enriquillo, the biggest salt-water lake in the Caribbean, which lies below sea level, and marvelled at the enormous iguanas who came to meet us after we had parked the car. We drove up into the mountains so I could see where Danilo had been brought up, and met friends of his father. They were making charcoal, just as his dad used to. It was the main fuel supply for cooking. Trees would be cut down and the green wood piled into a pyramid. A hole would be left in the middle, into which a very dry piece of wood would be inserted. The pyramid would be covered with soil and the dry stick in the middle lit. The pile of wood would burn slowly for up to five days until the end result was a large pile of charcoal.

One of his father's friends was called *El viejo*, which means the old man. He invited us into his little house and made me coffee. He roasted fresh beans in a pan, together with some sugar, and crushed them in a *pilon*, or pestle and mortar. Then he put them into a sort of muslin bag on a stick and poured boiling water through them, and added more sugar. Although it took an hour to make, it was the most amazing coffee I have ever tasted in my life.

I wanted to go to the toilet, and whispered to Danilo as I was not sure if there was a latrine. He pointed in the direction of a little hut at the bottom of the garden. I walked gingerly over, picking my way over the rocks and avoiding the chickens, and cautiously pulled open the rotting wooden door. There was an upturned crate with a hole in it and I hovered uncomfortably above it, grateful I always had a wad of toilet paper in my pocket. At the side of this tiny hut, on the ground, were a pile of corn on the cob, but no corn just the husks.

When I left the latrine I questioned Danilo about them. "Do people eat corn when they're sitting on the toilet? Is it some Dominican tradition I haven't heard of?" He looked at me blankly. "What you say?"

"Well, there was a pile of empty husks in the toilet," I explained.

He still looked blank and as realisation dawned, he howled with laughter, "Those *tusas*. You use to wipe bottom. Is toilet paper. Is very good toilet paper." Apparently the corncobs are given to the chickens who eat the corn, and the cobs are stacked in the latrine to be used as required. I didn't try one.

We had a lovely time in Barahona and I could see why it had such a special place in his heart. It was very different from the tourist resort we lived in, and I loved having seen a completely different side to the island. Whilst I loved the ocean, I could certainly see the attraction of living in the mountains.

Latin America has the highest levels of income inequality in the world and this is reflected in the Dominican Republic. According to the CIA factbook, 42% of the population lives below the poverty line and the next 40% are not much better off. The World Bank states that the top 20% of the population share 54% of the income.

Poverty is reflected in housing, lack of water (only 36% of homes have running water according to the 2010 Dominican Republic Census), lack of electricity, hunger and malnutrition. From 1940 to 1989 UNICEF states that 265,000 Dominican children died of malnutrition. The problem continues through life. There is food, but it is expensive relative to income levels. More than 2 million Dominicans live on less than $2 US a day – for everything, not only food.

Children usually start school at age 5, or nearly 6, with class sizes between 15 and 40 pupils. Every year there are exams and, apart from in the first few years when there is automatic progression, if they fail them they have to retake the year. According to Unicef, the repetition rate amongst the richest children is 2.3%, and amongst the poorest is 8.7%. If they make it to the 8th grade, they take national examinations known as the *Pruebas Nacionales*. There are four subjects: Spanish Language, Mathematics, Social Sciences and Natural Sciences and the pass rate is 65%.

Not everyone makes it to this grade. It is estimated that out of every 100 students who start school, only 53 finish 8th grade. They leave for a variety of reasons, and many do not even go to school. The main reason is money, as although the schools are more or less free (enrolment fee is about $1 US and examination fees the same), the children have to buy their uniform, back pack for their books, notebooks and pencils, and shoes. In some areas they also have to pay for their books, and as the books double as workbooks they are not reusable and can add significant expense.

Apart from those who live close by, they have to pay for transport – usually a *motoconcho*, although in some areas there are free school buses. Some will also drop out to work and it is estimated that 9% of children are involved in some form of child labour, although this tends to be mainly boys and more in the countryside than in the towns. Some of the girls will drop out as they become pregnant – teenage pregancies being a big problem in this country.

Following 8th grade there begins year 1-4 of high school ending with the exams for *Bachiller* which qualifies as university entrance. Not all schools offer high school education, so often the children must go to a different school much further away. The *Bachiller* consists of more exams than the *Pruebas Nacionales* and includes English, French, Civics, and Human Development. The exams tend to be multiple choice, which may be a reason why not many Dominicans can actually write very well. Many adults did not have the chance to finish their schooling when younger, and so now they go back to school by attending nightschool, or distance learning in order to graduate. Of all the children who start school only 12% will graduate from high school.

CHAPTER THREE
FAMILY LIFE

After about six months we moved out of the apartment, as it was not big enough for all of us. Not far away was a two-storey house with its own garden and an aged, gay Italian called Oscar living upstairs. He lived in Florida but used the house for holidays. Downstairs was a two bedroomed flat, much bigger than the apartment, and a large garden for Can Can. In the garden was a small house occupied by Chi Chi the security man or *watchyman* as it is called. Chi Chi was a nice man, short with enormous ears. He was a good handyman and knew everything about everything, from plumbing to electrics, to world politics, geography and even medicine. He would speak convincingly and you would believe him, as most Dominicans did. He and I would have long conversations.

"Lindsay, you have eight kidneys," he told me once.

"Really?" I replied, smiling. "And where is your liver?"

"Right here," he said pointing to under his left armpit. He was full of little gems like this. Like most Dominicans he was always known by his nickname, Chi Chi, 'little boy'. He had been brought up in the *campo*, 'village', usually very remote. His mother had died shortly after he was born; he was her fourth child and she was only fourteen years old. Whilst I often found it hard to comprehend the behaviour of the Dominicans I met, those from *campos*, known as *campesinos*, were even more removed from everything I was used to. Chi Chi's first sexual experience was when he was nine years old, he said – when he had sex with a donkey.

I continued to be amazed at how much Danilo would care for me. On Valentine's Day I came home from work, tired as usual, and Danilo grabbed me by the hand and dragged me into the house.

"Happy day of St. Valentin," he cried. "Now you go into bedroom." I dutifully walked down the corridor and gingerly opened the bedroom door.

"Wow!" I exclaimed. Everything was decorated in red. A red quilt cover, red lava lamp, red lampshade. And on the bed was a teddy bear with, 'I love you' on the front, and a mug with 'I love you' too. He came in behind me and put his arms round my waist.

"You like?"

"Yes, I love it," I said smiling, trying to take it all in.

Around this time Danilo joined the Dominican Air Force as a karate expert, because he had a black belt. Being military personnel meant he could not be arrested. Since we had been together he had been arrested three times for no reason; before we met he had never been arrested. The police knew he had a *gringa* (meaning foreign, usually American, but used for all foreign girlfriends) who they assumed had money, so they would arrest him and I would have to pay vastly inflated prices to get him out of jail. The last time he was arrested, in Guayacanes, the fishing village next to Juan Dolio, the police came to let me know and offered to give me a lift to the jail on their motorbikes to release him. They were hoping for a cut of the money I would have to hand over. Three bikes set off along the motorway and, as word got out, eleven motorbikes, each with two policemen, accompanied us to Guayacanes. I duly handed over the cash and Danilo was released, while the policemen jostled with each other to get their cut.

The police were very poorly paid and always asking for handouts or food, or money for petrol for their motorbikes. For some reason I didn't think of this as corruption, but accepted it as a way of life.

I had arrived in the Dominican Republic in November 2002 and had a return ticket to Madrid for the beginning of November 2003. We decided to try and obtain a visa for Danilo for a holiday in the UK and go back for a couple of weeks before my ticket expired. The visa process is not easy, and we had to fill in lots of forms and provide a range of information. Danilo had to prove he would not stay in the UK and had to have money in bank accounts in the DR and to own a business or have a good job. All the forms were submitted to the British Embassy and after a couple of weeks he was called for an interview. We hoped the fact I worked in the DR and had a letter from Klaus to say I was leaving for two weeks holiday would also help, and we had a letter of invitation from my father, Squadron Leader Peter Firth (*El Coronel* Peter) as Danilo called him.

The interview seemed to go well, although I was not allowed to go in with him. He was recalled into the Embassy to pick up his passport, not knowing if he had been granted a visa or not. I was working next to the pool at the hotel Talanquera, and kept looking at my phone praying it would ring with good news. In the end, fed up with waiting, I called him. "Hey, it's me, have you got your passport? Have you got the visa?"

"They no give me visa," he said, sounding dejected.

"Why the hell not?" I demanded, angrily.

"They say no visa," he continued. My shoulders slumped and I put my head in my hands. I was very disappointed. I had not realised that when you are with a Dominican, you too are imprisoned on the island as you cannot go anywhere with them. I was used to travelling wherever and whenever I wanted. Dominicans had to have a visa for almost everywhere in the world, and visas were very difficult to obtain. I wanted so much to show him England, to meet my family. I trudged back to my hut and there, sitting chatting to Jason and Billy, was Danilo.

"What are you doing here?" I asked.

"I come give you passport," he answered, grinning.

"What the hell do I want to see your passport for?" I said, grabbing it angrily. And of course, there it was inside, taking up one whole page, a visa for England. This was another of his jokes. He and the kids were always playing jokes on me. Once they took the cat, wrapped her in a towel and spread ketchup over the top of the towel.

"Lindsay! Lindsay!" yelled Dany running towards me. "The cat dead! Look, she only have head left!" I looked up surprised at hearing the cat miaow.

"So, if she is dead, how can she miaow?" I asked. The jokes became a daily occurrence.

Over the next three weeks, every morning we would have to count down how many days to go. He got a suitcase and would pack it and unpack it every day. Clothes were chosen carefully, and every sentence began with, "When I am in England..."

The big day came and we went to the airport accompanied by twenty or so people, none of whom had ever been to the airport. We checked in and all of us went upstairs to the viewing area to look at the planes. Open mouths all around, and then when it was time for us to go and board, the kids struggled to hold back tears.

"*Papi*, you come back," stammered Alberto, his bottom lip quivering.

"Of course we're coming back," laughed Danilo, "and we will bring you lots of presents too." It seems to be a common belief here that when someone leaves the country they will never come back. Everyone had a hug and off we went.

We arrived at immigration and handed over our passports. The official checked Danilo's, looked up with a frown, and said, "This visa is false. Come with me." I started shaking, and felt physically sick. How the hell could the visa be false? It had been issued by the embassy.

"Danilo, what's happening?" I asked.

"Wait for me here," he ordered me calmly.

I walked over to a row of plastic chairs and sat down watching as they took him off to a small office to the side. I had no idea what was going on, and kept looking at my watch, terrified we would miss our flight. My head slumped into my hands and I could feel my heart pounding in my chest.

Finally Danilo appeared, smiling. He had had to pay $100 US. It appears this was a way of taking money from first time

Dominican travellers, who would be nervous and unsure, and it was to happen several times to other Dominicans we knew who were flying for the first time. It left a nasty taste in my mouth.

We sat on the plane and I went through all the buttons on the seat, and the video player and helped him to put on his seatbelt. We were flying Iberia with everything in Spanish, which made life easier. Just before we took off Danilo asked, "When will my mouth go round to under my ears?"

"What?" I asked incredulously.

"Chi Chi told me when you fly, it so fast all skin on your faces stretches and your mouth moves round to be under your ears."

"No, no, that won't happen," I reassured him through helpless giggles.

The flight was smooth, but I began to discover what an interesting time was ahead of us, especially when our dinner arrived. It was like Tigger trying to find what he enjoyed eating in the *Winnie the Pooh* books.

Danilos do not like smoked salmon (spat out immediately), honey-roasted chicken (what idiot puts sugar on chicken), kippers (disgusting), creamy soups (looks like vomit), and the list was never ending. However, luckily, Danilos do like Cadbury chocolate, all English fruit especially apples, and Indian food.

We arrived in England and walked up to the immigration desk. Danilo turned to me.

"How much do I pay her?" he asked nervously.

"Don't be silly," I whispered. "This is England. No corruption here."

The immigration lady was lovely and let me translate, wished him a good holiday and we were through in no time. However, as we went through the 'Nothing to Declare' customs channel, for the first time ever in my life I was stopped by customs and we, and our luggage, were searched. This was to happen every time we travelled together.

Although there was no need, Mum and Dad had driven to the airport to meet us. I walked through the double doors into the arrivals hall, anxiously scanning the sea of faces. And there they were. Tears welled up as I ran towards them, leaving Danilo pushing the trolley.

"Hello love!" said Dad, embracing me in a big bear hug. I couldn't speak, I was choked, and turned to beckon Danilo forward. He held out his hand to Mum first and then Dad.

"Plee to mee' you," he said in his best English, smiling at both of them.

We drove to my storage lock up to get some warm clothes for both of us, and my parents returned to Huntingdon while Danilo and I boarded the train to central London. We went to London as most of my friends were there, and I wanted Danilo to see the sights. It had been my home for twelve years before I left England. Being with Danilo in London was like being with a cross between ET and Crocodile Dundee. He had never been out of the Dominican Republic, never been on a train, seen an escalator, been in a lift, been on the tube – the list was endless.

We were staying in a pub called the Mad Hatter and Danilo would tell taxi drivers to take us to the Crazy Hat. On the way to the room we passed an automatic shoeshine machine in the corridor. He had to spend ten minutes checking how it worked and then used it at least five times a day.

My first priority was to have a bath. I had not had one since leaving the UK as everywhere I had been there were only showers. Danilo was dumbfounded seeing me get into hot foamy water. We had no hot water in our house in the DR, so he had no idea about baths, or hot water. He insisted on having a cold-water bath with bubbles, and after that he would have at least one bath a day, gradually increasing the temperature. Eventually I persuaded him to have a bath without wearing his underpants. He often showered in his underwear as it washed it at the same time.

We spent a fun filled week in London, walking everywhere and seeing most of the sights. He was disinterested in the historic sites, apart from Buckingham Palace; the main attractions were the shops. We went to Hamley's toyshop eight times. He also adored the street life. He was fascinated by the little green man who would flash when you could cross the road, and shocked by the prices. We went into a Versace sunglasses shop on Regent Street where he wanted to buy a pair of sunglasses, as Dominicans love labels.

"How much?" he asked the man in the shop.

"Those are £200 sir," the sales assistant replied deferentially. I translated £200 into pesos for Danilo. "*Dios!*" he exclaimed, "Many money!"

"But sir, you are wearing Versace sunglasses," the assistant pointed out. "They must have cost the same."

"This sunglass was 20 pesos in Santo Domingo," answered Danilo, pointing out the country was full of fake merchandise. I had to drag him out of there to stop him setting up a deal to bring suitcases full of fake sunglasses to the UK on a regular basis.

The remainder of the holiday was spent with my parents in the country, which he loved. It was cold and he could not get over 'white smoke' coming out of his mouth when he breathed out. He insisted on wearing three pairs of underpants each day, as Chi Chi had told him the cold would make his penis shrink. And he was astonished by the size of the carthorses, that horses wore coats and pigs had little houses. There were ducks on the duck pond, which he went to feed every day. He loved the supermarkets and spent hours going around with his basket, but he missed his plantains and *pacofish*. However much he enjoyed England, he really wanted to get home to the Dominican Republic.

Whilst we were in England it was the first time we had been together twenty-four hours a day for two weeks. We didn't argue and he didn't get on my nerves. Danilo just made me laugh. He learned more English, although kept getting the letter 's' confused, so sleeping became *leesping*, smoking was *mosking*. It was hard to keep a straight face.

When we returned, as is the custom, all of the Dominicans cheered when the plane landed, and for the next few months all I heard was, "When I was in England... ". "In England they...".

Shortly after we returned it was our birthdays. They were only four days apart and as I left for work in the morning, Danilo said, "Tonight we have party for birthday. You ask people to come, I sort party."

He would be thirty-four and I would be forty-eight. I thought I had better mention this, and asked "Danilo, do you know how old I will be?"

"No idea," he answered. "Same as me."

"Well, actually not," I hesitated. But before I could tell him, he interrupted. "It no matter, you are young. *No importa*, what age you have. Now go and let me make party."

I had no idea what would happen, as nothing at all had been arranged. I arrived home at seven o'clock and was stunned. The garden was decked out in blue and white balloons, tables and chairs with flowers and tablecloths, the barbecue was heating up, and there were women in the kitchen preparing food. Drinks were on ice. I had no idea he could organise things so well.

The only slight hiccup was when the cake arrived. A friend of Danilo's had been to pick it up by taxi as it was a large rectangular cake two feet by one foot, and covered with Dominican soft, creamy icing. The taxi had broken down on the way to the house and he had to finish the journey on the back of a motorbike. The icing had blown off in the wind and he was covered from his waist to the top of his head in sugary icing. We did the best we could to scrape it off him and back onto the cake.

It was a fabulous party, with Dominican music blasting out and everyone dancing in the garden, and a scrumptious barbecue with chicken, sausages and burgers, accompanied by rice and salads. The alcohol flowed, mostly rum and coke, but there was a top table for the important guests, from the Air Force and the police, and they had two bottles of Black Label whisky. They enjoyed themselves, but unfortunately the policemen were arrested the next morning for turning up drunk to work and had to spend a week in jail.

We decided to buy a *colmado*, a little convenience store, as Danilo's logic was everyone needs food. He wanted to work and be the breadwinner, but the basic wage, at $200 US a month, would not go far towards contributing. He felt the only way to contribute more was to own his own business. The *colmado* was called Mar Azul (literally blue sea) and open all hours. It sold basic food stuffs and you could buy as little as you liked – one bread roll, one clove of garlic, one olive and one cigarette. Many Dominicans and Haitians do not have fridges and would only buy enough for a day at a time. They were not able to save money; there was never enough to think of saving. If it was in their pocket they spent it and had to hustle for money until they were paid again. In the DR wages are paid on the 15th and at the end of each month. I was used to shopping for two weeks, or a week at a time, but if they did that the food would go within a day or two, and so they bought just enough for each day.

Danilo started off working there all the time, but could not work out that you kept the money you took to buy more stock. In the beginning he always had money, but the shop would gradually empty. In the end he worked it out, and I started working there on my days off and in the evening. It was a great place to be, always full of laughter. The television was constantly on, and it was effectively the local cinema. The music was turned up loud, people would start drinking the rum and the beer, and they would dance in the shop and outside as well – it turned into the local discotheque.

And people went to the shop to see Danilo. He was equally popular with Dominicans and Haitians alike. He was funny and always made them laugh, and the children adored him. He would arm wrestle with the Haitian construction workers giving them a bottle of beer if they beat him, played magic games with the kids and give them sweets. He would teach the tourists to dance. He was very generous and he would never see anyone go hungry or if someone had a severe financial problem he would always try to help them out.

One Mother's Day Danilo called me.

"Go to bar after work. I have present for you for day of Mother. Be there six o'clock."

I went to the bar, and waited and waited. As usual Danilo was late.

"Here is present," he said, grinning, as he handed me a banana. I took it, smiling.

"Why have you bought me a banana?" I asked.

"Open banana," he replied. I opened the banana gingerly.

"Oh my God!" I squealed with delight... inside the banana was a key.

At last, I thought, I had my very own *pasola*. And then I turned round. Outside the bar was a black Suzuki jeep with *Lindsay* written across the windscreen. There were also transfers of a Mexican on a horse. What was that all about? And Danilo explained. My nickname at the time was *Jefa*, the female equivalent of *Jefe*, meaning boss. Dominicans would shout across the street at me "*Hola jefa*", pronounced 'heffa'. You can imagine being called a heifer in the street was not something I relished. Danilo wanted to put a transfer of a cow on the car, so people would see it was the *Jefa*. There were no transfers of cows available, the closest he could get, was a Mexican on a horse.

I loved my car. It was a manual gearbox, which was rare as most cars were automatic. Unfortunately, Danilo would try to drive it. He had never driven any type of car before and had no idea how to change gear. In the end he could do first and second gear only and when he wanted to go backwards, he would put it in neutral and get out and push. Consequently it was not long before the car had all sorts of bumps and scratches, as he would push it into things.

Although there are driving licenses in the DR, very few people take driving lessons, or a test, before being issued with a license. Licenses were available on the black market, you could just buy one. And most people did not bother to do that. The only problem was, if it was checked it would not be registered in the computer.

Danilo never learned to drive, nor did most people. It did not appear there was a minimum age for driving either, as I would often see young kids behind the wheel. Although there were supposed to be laws against drunk driving and wearing a seat belt, there was little enforcement. A large percentage of people drove with a beer or bottle of rum in their hands. Driving was very precarious. It seemed no one used dipped beam, and in the end I had to stop driving at night as I could not see. People would drive far too close behind too, and there were always motorbikes coming past on the inside and outside of you.

If there was a speed limit I had no idea what it was, and often people would drive far too fast, especially in the torrential rain. And there was no MOT (braketag in the USA) or equivalent. How some of the cars managed to stay on the road I have no idea. Many were rusted, many had smashed windscreens, no lights, bald tyres, but all, of course, had fabulous sound systems – usually it was impossible to put luggage in the boot as it was full of speakers.

Although we were enjoying living in the house, when the gay Italian, Oscar, came back to the DR he would often be annoyed about something or other. Either the kids were noisy, or Can Can was barking too much. We decided it was time to buy our own house. It seemed a big step to take, but I was happier than I could remember and house prices were much cheaper than the UK. It didn't make sense to carry on paying $400 US a month in rent. Money was not an issue, as between us we were earning enough to live on day by day, and I had several endowments and savings plans.

Steve had also asked me for a divorce, and I decided not to fight him in court over money but let him keep our main house and savings. He agreed to give me our cottage in the country and a small settlement. His girlfriend was pregnant and as we had both moved on, it seemed best not to fight for more money. I still felt guilty about leaving him, and although it was painful to know he was going to have a child with someone else, I couldn't deny I was happy for him, and of course I was happy myself. It felt like absolution. I had done the right thing.

Chi Chi found the house, owned by another Italian, Fosco, who had decided to return to Italy with his wife, as he was suffering with ill health. It was situated in the woods only a few minutes behind the main beach road. Danilo took me to see it on the *pasola*. We turned off the main road and bumped along a dusty rutted track for a couple of minutes. We stopped in front of a big metal gate, with a beautiful flame tree in bloom outside it. I shouted at the small gate, which was inset into the larger one.

"Hello! *Hola*!"

An elderly Italian man, stooped with white hair, came slowly to the gate. "No Dominicano," he shouted.

"He is my boyfriend, *mi amigo, mi esposo*," I shouted back.

"Ah, okay, *bene*," he coughed and let us both in, ducking down as we stepped through the little gateway. The house was white, single storey with three bedrooms, two bathrooms and a small house at the back for a *watchyman*. There were beautiful black tiles on the floor, but it did feel low and a little dark inside. However, there was a large covered terrace outside and I was sure we would spend most time there. It had a pool and a lovely mature garden, full of trees, and the best feature was a large roof terrace. We walked up the stairs to the terrace, which was enormous.

"This," said Danilo, "is lovely house. We have parties on roof and I teach karate to chil'rens." The house was only $120,000 US and included everything.

"Alright, *esta bien*, we will buy this house," I replied.

The day of the move Danilo said to me, "You go new house, I bring things. You wait for me in new house."

"No," I replied. "We have to put everything in boxes and label them so we know where to put them, and I need to pack everything up."

"This Dominican Republic," he grinned, "no need boxes." I had no idea what he was talking about, but walked to the new house, along the dusty track, and wandered from room to room imagining how it would be. I couldn't stop smiling.

An hour later a pickup truck arrived, reversed into the drive and I screamed out, "What the bloody hell!"

Nothing was in boxes. The pickup was piled high with everything from the house. My clothes were mixed with the contents of the fridge. Tops had not been screwed on bottles and everything was covered with ketchup and mayonnaise, belts wrapped round salami, rice in knickers. It was a mess. The children arrived and started unloading, and once the truck was empty it went back for another load. It took all day, but everything was moved from one house to the other.

The children had been driving me crazy with the mess they made, and we decided they could live in the *watchyman*'s house. It was small but had a bedroom, living room and bathroom and they were delighted to have their very own house. I was delighted too, I had my own bathroom so hopefully toothpaste would last longer than a couple of days and the toilet seat would stay down.

I ended up where I started, owning a house, and living with a man. The difference was I had two kids, two dogs and one cat. The cat was Missy Moonanga (*misu* means pussy cat in Dominican Spanish). Danilo had come home one night when we were in Oscar's house and sat down to dinner. After about thirty minutes he jumped up.

"Shit, I forget something," he said, then ran outside, unlocked and lifted up the seat of the *pasola*. He brought in a tiny kitten, it could only have been two or three weeks old, nestling in the palm of his hand.

"Oh my God!" I exclaimed, jumping up from the table. "I need to get a syringe and some baby milk."

"No be estupid. This Dominican cat. Eat salami." He proceeded to give it a chunk of salami, which the kitten devoured. She was a terror and moved to the new house with us. Unfortunately she did not last long, as she spat at Can Can once too often and met a gruesome end. She was replaced by Matilda and Mauricio, who started the Feliz cat dynasty, and in time we ended up with twelve cats. As more were born, more were barbecued by our Haitian neighbours or killed by the dogs. By then, as well as Can Can, we had her daughter Fred, named after the French diving instructor as she was born on his birthday, and was half pit bull and half street dog, called *vira lata* which literally means dustbin turn over, as they are notorious for fishing in bins and tipping them up.

We quickly settled into the new house and soon employed a gardener called *Araña* (Spider), so called because he was very good at climbing the scaffolding on construction sites. He was an average gardener, an above average consumer of rum, and a superb thief. Over time most of our garden tools disappeared, including the lawnmower. His hours of work were erratic depending on how much rum he had consumed the night before.

No thanks to *Araña* the garden was beautiful. The small houseplants I'd had in the UK, like the rubber plant and the Christmas cactus, were enormous trees here in my DR garden.

The outside walls were covered with bougainvillea and hibiscus. There were coconut palm trees in the garden, which Danilo would pick, climbing like a monkey to reach them. As well as the flowering plants we had all types of fruit trees and Danilo walked me around the garden explaining each one.

"This one she is *Chinola* (Passion fruit). She grow very fast and make nice yoos, but men no drink yoos."

"Why don't the men drink the yoos, I mean juice," I asked.

"Because if they drink yoos, no can do sex," he replied. Dominicans apparently believe passion fruit juice causes impotence, although it doesn't stop them eating the fruit. He continued. "This is mango, this tree is *lechosa* (papaya), which is very good for bad tummy. This one is *limon*, this one *toronja* (grapefruit), and here she is *china* (sweet orange) and here *naranja agria* (bitter orange)."

"Why bitter orange?" I asked. "What do you do with it?"

"You wash meat," he replied.

"What on earth for?"

"Makes meat nice and stop bad smell from meat." He carried on and nodded in the direction of something growing low on the ground. "That is *auyama* (pumpkin)."

"What, that over there?" I said, pointing at it.

"No!" he yelled at me, grabbing my outstretched arm and putting it by my side. "No point with finger. If point *auyama* he die." I tried not to smile at yet another Dominican superstition.

The garden was also full of wild life as the house was located in the woods. There were a variety of birds, from the tiny hummingbird to horrid big black rooks. Occasionally we would have a visiting woodpecker, known as a *carpintero* (carpenter). There were lizards of all shapes and sizes, from tiny geckos up to some the size of baby crocodiles – well, about nine inches long.

Every morning I would go outside to drink my coffee and walk into a tropical paradise. At night the air was filled with the sounds of little frogs and cicadas, and the heavy scent of the flowers, mixed with the smell of charcoal from the Haitian and Dominican neighbours cooking outside their *casitas*.

In the summer we had tarantulas, especially after the rain when they would move out of their sodden houses. Furry and very big, they were the size of side plates and would appear out of nowhere. They are not poisonous, but I read they pull hair out of their bottoms and throw it like a dart – it can be itchy, a bit like fibreglass. Not that I stayed close enough for long enough to see that happen.

We had frogs which made an incredible amount of noise, and snakes too, from small thin whip-like black and green snakes, all the way up to red and black Boa constrictors, all of them non-poisonous. The nastiest insect was the centipede. Much bigger than the British variety, six to nine inches long and fat. They were red with long black hairs and if you stamped on their head their tail would whip up and sting you. I discovered the only way to deal with them was to drop something on them covering them completely, like a bread board or my Spanish/ English dictionary and leave them for Danilo to dispose of.

It was amazing to think I owned another house, and I was happier than I could have ever imagined. It had been three years since I left England and Danilo and I both gave each other what we needed. I wanted to enjoy the moment, have fun, be happy and be loved and cared for. Danilo treated me like a princess. His favourite line was, "Whatever Lindsay want."

He would cook, clean, take me anywhere I wanted to go, buy me presents. Do everything he could to make my life easier. He paid the bills, did the shopping, and half of the cooking. It was the little things I adored. He knew when we ate whole fish I didn't eat the eyes, and didn't like seeing the kids eat the eyes either, so he would always cut the head off my fish so I didn't have to see them. We had sardines once, and he spent hours taken their eyes out before he barbecued them. If something went wrong he would arrange to have it fixed. I had never felt so loved, cared for and pampered. He wanted to climb out of poverty, have someone to help with the kids, a chance to travel, to live in a nice house or apartment, and I delivered those. Together we made a good team, and we were happy. We had my income from working as a diving instructor and his from the *colmado* and the Air Force, which was plenty for us to live on month by month.

Nevertheless, many expats thought he was with me for my money, as they were used to seeing sankies in action, and I am sure that was part of the initial attraction, but I was with him for selfish reasons too. He said he had decided to stay with me because I was *tranquila*, 'peaceful', I did not argue, scream or shout, which is how some Dominican women behave. Except when things disappeared from the house.

Danilo never stole from me. If his family needed money he would pawn his jewellery. I decided not to try and analyse the reasons he was with me, rather just enjoy being happy and not worry about what people thought. Every night, before going to bed, I would prepare the coffee maker for the next morning, just as I had done in England. There I would sigh as I did it, preparing to get up at 6am, with a two-hour commute and a stressful day ahead. Here I would prepare the coffee maker with joy in my heart, looking forward to another bright and sunny day, full of laughter and living life to the full.

COLMADO IN SPANISH LITERALLY MEANS FULL TO THE BRIM, AND IS equivalent of a corner shop or a *7-Eleven*. They are everywhere, with some being tiny, no more than a little shack, and some a little larger. Sometimes they are simply the front room of a house. They are all stuffed full of merchandise and are open from early in the morning, between 7 and 8, to between 8 and midnight.

Colmados are not self-service and are usually staffed by the owner or members of his or her family. You ask for what you want, well you demand it, by screaming '*dame*', which means 'give me'. It doesn't matter if anyone else is being served, or if anyone else is in front of you, you just shout anyway. He or she who shouts loudest is served next.

In the *colmado* you can buy almost anything you need. Many things are sold loose, such as rice, flour, beans, sugar, salt, washing powder and things you might not expect like cornflakes, oil, vinegar, soya sauce. You just take a container in and they fill it up for you. There is no minimum limit on the amount, so you can buy say 5 pesos (13 cents US) of oil or salt or whatever. There are always vegetables available such as plantains, yellow bananas, yuca, green peppers, onions and potatoes, tomatoes and celery.

Meat is normally restricted to chicken, which is usually kept in a washing up bowl and comes together with its feet and neck. Of course you can just buy a part of the chicken, or just its feet, as they are cheaper than the rest of the chicken. You can also buy smoked pork chops, which for some reason come in a sort of muslin sock, and of course, salami. Most *colmados* will also stock salted cod called bacalao which, due to the fact it is heavily salted, does not have to be refrigerated and is stored in a wooden box. There are several tinned goods such as carnation milk, peas, sweet corn, and naturally beer and rum. Many items are also sold in tiny little packets, which cost from 1-10 pesos. There would include coffee, olives, bleach, vinegar, shampoo, shoe polish, ketchup and tomato paste.

A large percentage of people buy on credit and carry around a little piece of cardboard with what they owe on it, torn off a packet of something. Then when they get paid on the 15th or the 30th, or the 25th for government jobs, they take their piece of cardboard to the *colmado* and pay it all and then are given another torn off scrap of cardboard for the next two weeks or month.

As well as being the main place for food, the *colmado* doubles up as a bar at night – and all day Sunday – and is the main social centre of the neighbourhood. There is usually a television in one corner and the *colmado* fills up for baseball games and the daily soap opera programmes. Even though the television is on, that does not stop the constant blare of *merengue* and *bachata* ringing out from the 4-foot tall speakers, positioned at the entrance of the shop. At night everyone gathers and sits on the ubiquitous plastic chairs and drinks beer and rum. If there are not enough chairs then they use upturned plastic beer crates. There will often be at least one noisy game of dominoes in progress, and the customers are often accompanied by their dog or fighting cockerel who sits quietly under the table amongst all the revelry.

WHAT ABOUT YOUR SAUCEPANS?

CHAPTER FOUR
MAKING IT PERMANENT

LIFE WAS BUSY. IT WAS 2004, I WAS STILL WORKING AS A DIVING instructor and had been there two years, although it seemed much longer. Fred and Neil had both left, Fred had gone to Vietnam and Neil back to corporate life in the UK, but more instructors had arrived. Ian, Welsh with shaggy blonde hair, looking like the archetypal diving instructor, and his girlfriend Birge, a very attractive German who spoke perfect English.

Danilo was in the *colmado* some of the time and whilst still in the Air Force he did extra work for the DNI – the Department for National Investigations – a cross between the FBI and the CIA. He worked a couple of nights a week hunting down drug dealers, illegal immigrant traffickers and paedophiles. He was basically a spy. It was not a high paying job, but double the average salary and it meant he had good relationships with the police, which is always useful in the DR.

He became friendly with high-ranking people in the Air Force and DNI, generals and colonels and such, and they would often come over to the house for dinner. Danilo was very good at his job as he knew so many people in Juan Dolio who would keep their ears to the ground and tell him what was going on. Most of them lived in the shacks in the woods, although not all, and our house became a major meeting point. I began to call his friends 'dwendies', which is taken from the Spanish word for garden gnome, *duende*. I would wake up in the morning and wander outside in my dressing gown and there would be four or five Haitians and Dominicans sitting in my garden, like gnomes without the fishing rods. They would hang around most of the day, and if they did not turn up during the day they would arrive in the evening when dinner was being served. I would cook for ten rather than five.

I gave them all numbers. Number one dwendy was Saya. He had known Danilo for years, and used to help to look after his children when Danilo was working in Santo Domingo.

"Why doesn't Saya work?" I asked Danilo,

"He has no *cedula*," he replied. The *cedula* is the Dominican identity card issued at eighteen.

"Why doesn't he have a *cedula*?" I persisted.

"Because when he was small his father sold his birth certificate to an illegal Haitian. No birth certificate, no *cedula*. No *cedula*, you no can work."

There were about twenty dwendies altogether. They would come and go depending on what opportunities came their way. On the one hand, it was nice to have the house full of people and laughter, but on the other, I longed for peace and quiet and occasionally got frustrated at feeding the five thousand.

As well as the dwendies, people came to the house to ask for help, and Danilo would turn no one away.

"Danilo, please let me have 500 pesos to stop my motorbike being repossessed."

"Danilo, can you lend me 1,000 pesos to get my jewellery out of the pawn shop?"

"Danilo I need 500 pesos to buy medicine for my daughter."

He rarely said no. Some did pay him back, most didn't. I began to learn that 'lend me' was 'give me'. We also helped with medical issues. Medicines were often given to me by tourists before they left the DR, and I would distribute these to local people who were sick. Although the medicines were available, many people could not afford to buy them. I would take blood pressure for pregnant women, and if it was high would send them to the doctor. I treated cuts, and minor burns, although sometimes I was faced with horrific burns where women had thrown hot fat or hot water over each other, fighting over men. I gave injections too – I had become used to injecting myself during IVF treatment. As there were no ambulances, the car was in constant use taking people to hospital after accidents, or when they were sick. Often it would be washed down after accidents on the highway or after someone had started to give birth in the back seat. We became accustomed to being woken up at two in the morning to take someone to the hospital in San Pedro.

One morning during breakfast Danilo said, "Lindsay you no need clean, have Angelita clean. Is only 5,000 pesos every month." He was right, it was about £100 a month and would make my life much easier. Angelita was a seriously large lady in her mid twenties who lived opposite us in a little wooden shack. Although she was born to Haitian parents, she had been born in the DR, had a Dominican *cedula* and was technically Dominican. She had six children by four different fathers, none of whom were currently with her.

Everything started well, and she was a great worker. She would work for six days a week, starting at ten in the morning making the beds and washing the floors. Floor washing is a complex business consisting of flooding the house to start, and then the water is mopped up using a *suape* (mop) and rung out into a bucket. Local disinfectant (*mistolin*), which has a very strong smell, is added to water. One gallon would last six months in England, but in the DR it lasts a week as so much is used. This is done every day, whether the floor is dirty or not. Angelita would clean the bathrooms and do the laundry in our twin tub, which was plastic and lived outside. She would use too much washing powder and insist on putting *chloro* (bleach) in with the clothes with the result they all changed colour and rotted quickly.

However, things started to go missing. Bottles of Coca-Cola, knickers, T-shirts, shoes, a frozen chicken, plates, sheets, cups, glasses. The final straw was when I came home one day and my sofa had gone. Angelita had to go. She was quite blasé about going as I had to pay her a couple of months salary as redundancy pay, known as *liquidacion*.

I asked Danilo, "Can she not see how silly she is? Now she will have no job, and she cannot understand that stealing is wrong."

"She no see stealing," he replied. "We has money, she no has. We friend so she take from us. Not stealing."

By now I was so used to things disappearing, the fury I previously felt when things went missing had diminished, although not completely disappeared. I had other sofas, and she had none – I was learning to share. Angelita continued to live in her hut opposite us and gradually her one hut became forty huts, each with a family. When we moved into our house there were maybe fifty Haitians living in huts close to us, and this increased rapidly over the years to several hundred, especially after the earthquake. If you went into Angelita's hut it was full of things from my house. I had no idea she had taken so much. We stayed friendly with her, and I would pay for school uniforms for the children each year, helped out with food sometimes, and medical supplies.

The lack of thinking through the consequences of actions today was a recurring theme across all walks of life in the DR, from doctors and lawyers, to the unemployed living in the shacks. Time and time again professionals would overcharge me, and most expatriates. It was more important to have money today than establish a trustworthy relationship, which would bring far more money in the long term. There was a definite dual pricing system, a price for Dominicans and a price for foreigners. Although I could understand prices would be based on someone's ability to pay, it did sometimes leave a nasty taste when I felt I was being ripped off. Luckily, I had Danilo to do much of the negotiating for me, and the longer I was in the DR, and the better I spoke Spanish, the less it happened.

There was also a system of commission. If you recommended someone to a lawyer or a plumber or electrician, anyone, the person who carried out the work would pay you commission. We had arranged to have some metal bars installed at the windows in a new room we had built as an outside office for me, and I paid the man the deposit. He finished the work and stood in front of me and Danilo as I handed over the final payment.

"There you go," I said. "20,000 pesos as agreed." He took the money, counted it, and handed Danilo 2000 pesos.

"*Tu comision*, Danilo," he said. I looked a bit blank. Danilo turned to me. "And here your half Lindsay," he said, giving me 1000 pesos.

The jeep was fine, but Danilo was still having trouble with gears, and we needed something bigger – ideally a car each. We looked at several second-hand ones, but in the DR most people buy a car on hire purchase, and when they cannot make the payments – and before it is repossessed – they take as much out of the car as they can. Cars only a few months old had no seat belts, no door handles, no lights and it seemed silly to pay a lot of money for something like that. In the end we bought a new automatic Mitsubishi pickup, which was perfect. Danilo could drive it, although it didn't take long before it accumulated dents and scratches as he continued to drive into things.

For our first Christmas, Danilo had taken the children to a *campo* up in the hills above the town of Bani, an hour the other side of Santo Domingo, to be together with Christian. I didn't go as I had to work, nor was I allowed to see Christian. Christian had now left for Spain and this year, in our new house, would be our first Christmas together as a family. I wanted to make it memorable and for Danilo and the boys to have an English Christmas as well as a Dominican one. I talked to Danilo about it.

"What do you think we should do this Christmas?" I asked. "Tell me what you're used to doing."

"I never have Christmas when child as no one know what day it is. No one know what month it is in mountains. No Christmas and no birthday ever."

"But didn't you ever have presents?" I asked, astounded.

"What present? Nothing to buy in mountains. All I ever

want was machete like my father have. My boys never have presents, no money for presents."

We eventually agreed Danilo would cook Dominican dinner on Christmas Eve, and I would prepare a traditional English Christmas lunch on Christmas Day. We would open presents on Christmas Day rather than waiting until 6 January, Three Kings Day (Epiphany), when Dominican children traditionally have presents.

I sat the children down. "Santa Claus is a man who comes from the North Pole where it is very cold and he brings the good children presents," I explained. "You have to write a list of what you want him to bring you. As we have no fire we'll have to put it on the barbecue and the smoke will take your list to the North Pole."

"He has camels," explained Dany to Alberto. "He has a lorry which is pulled by camels." Seeing as I had no idea of the Spanish word for reindeer, we stuck with camels.

"I want peanut butter," piped up Alberto.

"I want a *poloshe* (T-shirt)" said Dany.

"Me too, I want a *poloshe*," yelled Alberto, and they ran off to get paper and pencils to make their lists. Dany wanted jeans, a T-shirt and a pencil. Alberto wanted jeans, a T-shirt and a jar of peanut butter. They had never had toys and did not think of them. They really believed, well I thought they did, although they were in their teens by now. On Christmas Eve Danilo cooked crab, chicken and goat. The crabs he had bought the day before and put them in the sink – alive. Half had escaped, and for days afterwards I found crabs under the beds, in the wardrobes and cupboards. The goat arrived, but not in a nice Sainsbury's plastic tray, but whole, with fur and hooves and eyes and ears. I made myself scarce as Danilo and the dwendies sharpened their machetes to get it ready for the pot.

For the Christmas Eve feast, Danilo invited the dwendies and their families, and many of the poor people who lived locally. There were over a hundred people in the garden. *Araña* was drunk and kept falling asleep in his food, Angelita had a plastic bag on her lap and shovelled food and knives and forks and glasses into it, and there was a queue of people at the gate asking for food for themselves and their families. When everyone had left, the kids hung up their stockings and left out a carrot for the camels and a glass of rum for Santa Claus. When I woke up early the next morning to fill their stockings, there was a note to Santa Claus.

"Dear Santa Claus. We thought you might smoke Marlboro light and drink *Brugal* (local rum). Love from Dany and Alberto." There was a packet of cigarettes and a bottle of rum. It looked like they had sussed out Santa Claus.

It was a great Christmas. The kids had bought me all the things which had disappeared during the year such as knives (used instead of screwdrivers by everyone and never returned), shampoo ('borrowed' to wash coloured clothes as the washing powder has bleach in it), glasses (broken on a daily basis) and mugs. Danilo bought me clothes. Dominican hooker clothes, about all you can buy apart from in the up-market malls in the major towns. Very tight jeans and low cut tops and 'follow me, fuck me' shoes. It is a tradition to wear new clothes on Christmas Day, so I served the English Christmas lunch tottering around on high heels dressed like a hooker. They were speechless at the turkey, never having seen one before, and although I was hoping to make turkey soup afterwards, I went into the kitchen to find Angelita and one of the dwendy's wives fighting over the turkey carcass, with a tug of war between them. In the end I cut it up and gave them half each.

It was a different Christmas, but my best Christmas ever – watching the pleasure on everyone's faces and, most of all, those of the children.

My parents celebrated their 50th wedding anniversary on 1 January 2005, but had planned a big family party for the following April. Danilo obtained another visa, and we went on our second trip to the UK. This time we planned to stay at my parents for most of the trip, with a visit to the north of England so he could see a bit more of the country.

The party was held in a village hall, with nearly a hundred of my relatives, and Danilo was able to meet most of my extended family. We wandered through the room talking to friends and relatives, some of whom I had not seen for years. Danilo was the centre of attention – he was charming and they all fell in love with him immediately.

A three-course lunch had been prepared by my aunt and one of my brothers, Peter, who was a chef, and after we had eaten Mum asked me to make a speech. She wanted me to mention other people in the room who had something to celebrate that year, which I did. As I was speaking, I decided as I was mentioning everyone else, I may as well announce that Danilo and I had decided to get married in only six weeks time.

Danilo had not gone down on one knee, but it was something we both knew would happen eventually. I was now firmly settled in the DR, we had a lovely relationship, never argued, simply tried to help each other. To be honest I was not concerned about getting married again, but it was very important to Danilo, it was a status symbol to be married, usually something only the wealthy Dominicans did. Once my divorce had been finalised in February he decided on the date, and came home one day and suggested 20 May, 2005.

I wish I could say everyone was delighted for us, but whilst no one said anything, I could tell there was not universal approval at his announcement. No one from the UK would be coming to the wedding, apart from my best friend Sue, who was to be the *madrina* (a female best man). I don't think it was a snub that other friends or family didn't come, as we'd given people very little time to make travel arrangements. I was to be given away by a *padrino* (godfather), and this was to be José Tomas Perez, the Senator for the National District in Santo Domingo, a senior politician who would become candidate for his party's Presidential nomination. Over the past year or so, Danilo had become involved in politics and our witnesses at the wedding were two local party members who had asked José Tomas to be the *padrino*, and he had agreed.

The date was set and unlike my first wedding, I had nothing do as Danilo arranged everything. It was a delight to have everything organised for me, from shopping, to paying the bills, and now to planning the wedding. The venue was Guavaberry Beach Club, a perfect setting, only a few minutes from our house. The wedding was to be at 5.30pm, when it was cooler, followed by music and dancing and finally the food. You always eat late at Dominican weddings, or any type of party, as people leave as soon as they have eaten – most only come for the food.

It is not traditional to have a wedding present list. People bring presents if they want to. I wanted to buy Danilo a wedding gift, and I knew he wanted another dog. A big dog. I phoned the local vet's office and they had a three-month-old male Great Dane, and delivered the dog, who I named Tyson, to the *colmado* a couple of days before the wedding. For three months old he was enormous, all ears and legs. However, when it came time to take him home he refused to walk and sat down in the road. In the end we managed to get number two dwendy, Ezequiel, to carry him home. We arrived at the house where Danilo was outside.

"Here is your wedding present," I announced proudly. He walked over with a big expectant smile on his face and then his face dropped and he asked, "Why you buy me goat?"

"This is no goat, this will be a very big dog. A *Gran Danes*," I explained.

He was delighted telling everyone he had a Great Dane à la King. I had no idea where the 'à la King' came from until I picked up Tyson's pedigree certificate and saw he was a Harlequin Great Dane. Tyson slept by the side of our bed at night, breaking the rule about dogs in the house until he couldn't fit, and then he moved outside with Can Can and her daughter Fred. Fred quickly became enamoured with Tyson and went on to have a litter of puppies with him, born on his first birthday.

The day of the wedding dawned with perfect weather. When José Tomas arrived the 120 guests stood and cheered. I don't think anyone noticed my entrance, they were far more impressed with him. The Dominicans are very deferential towards people in authority, particularly politicians. He very generously gave us a microwave as a wedding gift. The service was traditional, at least I think it was, as it was conducted in Spanish. The judge wanted to make sure she omitted nothing with José Tomas being there. I had to say '*yo accepto*' (I do) after each phrase. I must have *accepto*-ed fifty times and had no idea what most of them were. We had two political witnesses too, *Licenciado* Franklin Compres, and *Ingeniero* José Luis Bencosme.

How do I describe *Licenciado* Frankin Compres? *Licenciado* means he had a degree. As the Dominicans are very proud of their titles they use them all the time. He was short, with a very strong resemblance to Bluebottle from the *Goon Show*. He had been a party member for years and knew all of the ins and outs of the political system. He was married to Prieta, meaning 'black woman', and they lived in a small block-built house off the main street in Guayacanes, the fishing village next to Juan Dolio. They had four children, and Compres had a weakness for whisky, the casino and leaving his wife, which he did periodically when she would attack him with a frying pan after yet another night at the casino. He was always well dressed, and drove a beat up Honda. He was a nice man when not full of whisky, but a diabetic who would often have sugar attacks, which would lay him low for a few days.

Ingeniero (Engineer) José Luis Bencosme was also heavily involved in politics and very ambitious. Although he lived in the capital he was often in Guayacanes, as there was talk they were going to split it away from San Pedro and make Guayacanes and Juan Dolio into their own municipality. If that happened we would need a Mayor, and José Luis wanted the job. He was involved in the local political scene and looking for the support of my *padrino*, José Tomas, to help get the position.

It was a fabulous wedding. Danilo had done an outstanding job arranging it. Everywhere looked stunning with large and colourful Caribbean flowers and candles. We had a live band and the local 'Michael Jackson' performed, miming to MJ's songs with all the movements right down to the crotch clutching. The drink flowed and the food, when it appeared, was delicious. The main dish was goat stew, traditional at weddings, but we also had fish, prawns, rice and a whole range of different salads. Each table had a glass goldfish bowl with candles inside, and Danilo had put flaming torches all along the beach. As the sun set the whole venue was bathed in flickering candlelight. We did all the traditional things – the first waltz, Danilo pulling my garter off with his teeth and I tossed my bouquet. Two women fought over it, grabbing for the flowers as it fell and had a catfight over the remnants on the floor. They ended up dishevelled and the bouquet was in tatters. It tipped it down with rain from about eight o'clock onwards, which is apparently a blessing on the marriage, and at eleven o'clock we left and spent the night in a local hotel.

I was married again. This time my name was Mrs Happy. Traditionally I should have taken my maiden name and his name but that would have been too difficult for Dominicans to pronounce and I used 'de' meaning 'of' so I was Lindsay de Feliz. I was deliriously happy and could see no reason why that would ever change.

I had left my job with the dive school just before we went to the UK in April, as I needed to work more hours in the *colmado*, and I really enjoyed it. We also employed Jason and Billy who had worked with me. At first it was hard for me to serve people as I had no idea what they wanted for instance:

Fa – fab = washing powder

Geelay – Gillette = razor blade

Cotay – Kotex = sanitary towel

Sanwee – sandwich

Una fria – literally 'a cold one' = beer

And the Haitians who had recently arrived and could not speak Spanish would ask for everything in Creole.

At the same time Danilo was spending more time with José Luis Bencosme and Franklin Compres involved with politics, as well as his DNI work. Although we never argued and had a great relationship, some aspects of Dominican culture continued to frustrate me. Danilo seemed to have no concept of time. There were only three time periods, five minutes, which was up to an hour, twenty minutes, which was up to two hours, and an hour, which was all day. If he went out I would ask how long he would be and he would say he would be back later.

When he went to work for the DNI it was worse, as he would say he would be back at ten o'clock at night and turn up at ten o'clock the following day. To be fair, the lack of timekeeping was certainly not something only Danilo did – everyone seemed to do it. Meetings would always be late, visitors would always be late. If you were expecting someone at two o'clock, you would call them at three o'clock and they would say, "*Estoy llegando*", 'I am arriving'. What it means is, "I am now thinking of leaving my house two hours away." The only way I found to cope with the timekeeping was to accept it. If we had people coming for dinner I'd cook something, which would not spoil if eaten late. As far as Danilo was concerned, we agreed dinner was at 7.30 every night and if he could not make it back for then, he would call me. Otherwise I did not need to know when he would be back. This worked perfectly and he would always call if he would be late for dinner.

The second issue was the inability to answer any question directly, which again did not only apply to Danilo but to many Dominicans. A typical conversation would be,

"Where is the car?"

"It is on its way."

"No, I want to know where it is."

"It won't be long."

"Where is the car now?"

"Around."

"Where is the bloody car!"

If he had been for a meeting, I would ask what had happened and the answer was always in English, "Everything is okay."

"Yes, but what happened in the meeting?"

"Everything is okay." It was frustrating as I was used to being part of decision making, and whilst of course I did not understand how things worked in the DR, I still wanted to be informed and involved. I would say, "Danilo, I want to be involved, I'm not stupid and maybe I can help."

"This is Dominican Republic and this is man things, women no talk man things, women talk women things," would be his reply.

"Well, maybe Dominican women talk women things, but English women talk man things too," I would reply in frustration.

My mother told me my father had a chest infection. Dad was studying Spanish at the Open University and had nearly finished his degree. His Spanish was much better than mine and he had been to see me once on his own, and once with Mum. He loved Danilo and the pair of them got on really well. Danilo called him Papa, as his own father, Juan had died a few years previously. Danilo still missed his father desperately, and if ever we talked about him, he would well up with tears.

Dad's chest infection did not clear up and he was treated for bronchitis. He was admitted to hospital and fluid drained from his lung. On a Friday in October Mum called and said he had been diagnosed with lung cancer, but it was not life threatening. It was a shock, but I was not too concerned as she explained cancer grows more slowly the older you are and Dad was 72. The following Monday she called again.

"Lindsay, you need to get home as soon as you can. Your father has been diagnosed with mesothilioma. He's not good.

Please just get home. You need to come home." I booked a flight immediately and left the following day, arriving in in England on the Wednesday morning.

I was too late. Dad had died the previous evening. I was numb. I'd had no chance to talk to him. No chance to tell him how much I loved him and how grateful I was for his support. He had never been ill in his life, and it had happened so quickly it felt like he had been killed in an accident. It felt bloody unfair. He seemed fine when we had seen him a few months before at the anniversary party. Although he had not been a big part of my life as I was growing up, as he was often away, over the last few years we had grown closer, especially after I had left the UK. I was devastated.

I spent two weeks with Mum, and whilst it was a terribly sad time, it was lovely to be back, eat all the favourite foods I missed like dumplings, lamb chops, blackberry and apple crumble, cream, speak English and watch English television. Danilo could not come with me as there was not enough time for him to get a visa. Visas only lasted six months and then another had to be applied for. It was very hard. My brothers, twins who were six years younger than me, were there with their wives, and my younger sister Elisabeth was there with her American husband. I sat talking with Elisabeth one evening.

"I wish Danilo could be here. It's horrid he can't just jump on a plane like everyone else."

"I know, it must be," she sympathised. "It's hard enough for us having to fly in from America, but at least we can do it." We all lived far away. Elisabeth and Gary in America, Patrick, his wife and three sons in Guernsey, and Peter, his wife and two boys in the Isle of Skye. We were concerned about leaving Mum, but she appeared to be coping well, as she had always been independent, and whilst all of us children lived far away, she had her sister and plenty of friends in the area. I did feel bad about leaving her though, and Danilo insisted she should come and live with us. For a Dominican it was unheard of for someone's mother to live by themselves, let alone in a different country, as family is so important. However, she wanted to stay in her own house and I think it would have driven her mad living in the DR.

In several ways I was moving steadily out of my comfort zone. Things that had previously been important to me, no longer were. I rarely wore makeup, or designer clothes, preferring instead vest tops and combat trousers, with the latter there was no need for a handbag. I didn't mind if the new car was scratched, which was just as well as Danilo seemed to make a habit of hitting things. I still had my jeep, but dwendy number one, Saya, was also driving it and had several accidents, usually caused by him thinking that one metre from the car in front was sufficient stopping distance.

I loved the personal freedom – not having to wear a helmet on a motorbike, being allowed to smoke anywhere, music in the shops, dancing in the streets. I loved the easy way of life. If I forgot my keys and was on the beach I could phone a *motoconcho* and he would go and get them and deliver them to me on the beach. All sorts of services would come to the house. The rag and bone man, the scrap metal man, the vegetable man, the live chicken man, the medicine man, and the ice-cream man. They would pass most days shouting through a megaphone what was on offer that day. I still loved the friendliness and the optimism and the general aura of happiness.

But many things were beginning to become frustrating. The house was always full of people, which was nice, but the more people in the house the more things disappeared, especially food, but also other items such as plates and glasses and linens. Having so many people to cook for became wearing, as well as expensive. Culturally it was acceptable when you went to someone's house to walk inside and help yourself to food and coffee. I could never imagine that happening in the UK, and I cannot deny I found it hard to accept. Danilo could not understand how, in all my years of living in London, I never had unexpected visitors at the door. Of course people would come to see you, but it was always prearranged.

Our electricity was often out, as so many Haitians were now plugged into our line, and in the end we paid for our own transformer (nearly a year in the installation process), which delivered reliable electricity, much more than many places in the DR had. Occasionally the load would be too much and the transformer would blow up. When that happened, everything that was plugged in would blow up too. Televisions, coffee makers, stereo. This happened once and we needed a new television. Klaus had one he was prepared to sell to me and I called Danilo.

"Danilo, I have a television but it is bigger than the one we had. It's thirty inches wide. Can you check to see if it'll fit?" We had a unit in the bedroom with a space in the middle for a television.

"It fit," he replied immediately.

"Well, have you measured it? There's no point in having it if it won't fit."

"It fit," he insisted. He came and picked up the television.

When I got home, there was the television snugly placed in the unit. It looked fabulous, until I noticed there was a massive chunk missing out of the side of the cupboard. It had not fitted, Danilo had used a machete to make it fit.

Dominicans always managed to solve problems in whatever way they could, using whatever was available. If the car battery did not work the contacts would be cleaned with half a lime. If the electric car windows were stuck, melted butter would be poured in. Rocks took the place of hammers, knives the place of screwdrivers.

I thought if you had not owned material things, once you did have them you would look after them. What I did not understand was, if you had never been taught, you didn't know how to look after or appreciate them. In the DR nothing seemed to last long. It was not only that things were not looked after, but the constant surges in electricity, the humid climate, and proximity to the sea, ruined all metal appliances. In the last few years I have got through three twin tub washing machines, four liquidisers (the kids put ice in them to make juice, and they crack), one boiled egg maker, three toasters, two toasted-sandwich makers, four complete cooking knife sets (not just taken as screwdrivers but also used to cut wires, mend cars, dig the garden, kill centipedes – you name it), and two cookers. The list was endless, but in England you would have something for years and years, but here it was only a few months. Also, what you thought were new items were often rejects from other countries; when you opened your new microwave and looked at the instruction book, the guarantee page would be stamped, 'Guarantee Null and Void'.

I felt I had moved from the first phase of seeing the country through rose coloured glasses, to understanding and experiencing more. I certainly felt frustrated as I tried to understand the culture and let go of my preconceived ideas of how things should be, and tried to accept the way of life here and understand why people were the way they were.

On the whole life continued to be one long holiday. I was busy with the *colmado* and new and old friends. There was an English girl called Sue from Liverpool, who had bought a bar locally – Freedom Bar, and I would often go there for a chat. We had known each other for a couple of years as she was the tour representative in Hotel Talanquera where I used to work, and she had a Dominican boyfriend too.

I had an American friend, Margaret, from Charleston, South Carolina, who lived in the up-market gated community nearby. Her husband, Terry, worked in the Free Zone, an area where tax-free factories produce goods such as clothing and jewellry for export.

Margaret, who was the same age as me and great fun, had never lived outside America before coming to the DR and it was a huge change for her. I had met her in Freedom Bar and we had the same sense of humour so I offered to take her shopping. She did not have a car and was a little concerned about taking the local buses as she didn't speak Spanish. I picked her up in the jeep, which had been fixed, to a point, but the windscreen was still shattered, although you could just about see through it, and there were no seat belts. She came to the door dressed in capri pants and a nicely ironed shirt, with her long blonde hair neatly tied back in a ponytail and nearly had a heart attack when she saw the jeep. I took her to San Pedro de Macoris where there is a local indoor market. The smell is incredible and is like a scene from *Blade Runner*, with narrow alleyways, stalls on both sides selling meat and fish covered with flies, fruit and vegetables, herbs and spices, sacks of rice, the obligatory voodoo shop with its lotions and potions, and lots of shouting and screaming.

Margaret and I would often spend time together, walking on the beach, going shopping, or I would sit on her posh patio, looking out at the beautifully manicured golf course and munching my way through the American goodies she would bring back from the States on one of her trips home. It was lovely for me to be able to spend time speaking English and being with people of a similar culture.

We would also meet up several evenings a week at Freedom Bar where we would sing karaoke together and have a few glasses of *Brugal*.

Unfortunately, before I knew it, life was to change dramatically.

LOANS ARE A BIG PART OF THE CULTURE, AS FEW PEOPLE EARN enough to save. If they want something it is bought on credit. Interest rates are high, around 100% a year or more, and if you miss one payment rates go higher.

Most loans are given by loan sharks, *prestamistas*, who will often ask for the bank ATM card. When wages are paid on the 15th and last day of the month, the loan sharks go to the bank machine with numerous cards. They take the month's wages for each client and give it to the owner of the card, minus what they owe on the loan. The rates for loan sharks are often more than 100%. They will usually give the client three months to pay a missed payment, and if they do not, the item the loan was for, will be repossessed. People are desperate to make a missed payment to save losing their car, motorbike or home.

The *compraventa*, or pawnshop, is also an important part of life, and people will pawn anything from jewellery to fridges, stereos, liquidisers. Again the interest rates are high although not as high as a *prestamista*. Usually items are held for four months, and if you cannot pay to redeem your item by then, you lose it.

CHAPTER FIVE
PARADISE TURNS TO HELL

Saturday, 21 July 2006, started much like any other day. I got up and fought off the army of cats, who were desperate for their breakfast. A little procession into the dining room to give them their food, all ten of them, switched on the coffee machine and went back into the bathroom for morning ablutions. I slipped on my flip flops and wandered outside in my pyjamas and dressing gown for the first coffee and cigarette of the day. It was already hot, in the mid 80s.

The workers began arriving to continue building the small two-bedroomed house we were constructing in the corner of the garden. We had bought the land adjacent to ours with the idea of building a new house for us, which would better meet our requirements than the house we were in, and also a small two bedroomed house for the children. They were typical messy teenage boys, Dany was seventeen now and Alberto fifteen, and I thought if they had their own little house maybe they would look after it. They were outgrowing the *watchyman* house, and we were thinking of having a live-in gardener so we would need the *watchyman* house anyway.

Today was to be the day for putting on the *plata* (concrete roof). To do this, a framework had been built of wood, and the concrete would be poured on top. Once the concrete has set, which takes a couple of days, the wood is taken away and hey presto you have a flat, concrete roof. No slates to fly off in hurricanes and no wood to get munched by termites. The concrete is mixed by hand in buckets and hauled up to the roof by means of a man on the roof with a rope. It has to be done quickly, and there were twenty Haitians or so working, far more than the usual three or four, under the supervision of the *maestro* (foreman), Chi Chi, he of the large ears, and a few gallons of rum. For some reason the putting on of the *plata* always involves rum. Although it is hard work in the hot sun, as it was a Saturday the men would only be working till noon. Construction employment rules are very strict in the DR, five and a half days a week, eight o'clock until five o'clock, finish at noon every Saturday and get paid every second Saturday.

Danilo came outside, he was heading to the Air Force base to practice karate.

"Danilo, here, take the bank book with you. You need to take out 90,000 pesos and make sure you bring it back here by noon to pay the workers," I instructed him, handing over the dog-eared cardboard bankbook. "And noon is noon. Twelve o'clock. Don't be late. English time, not bloody Dominican time." He took the book.

"I unnerstan. I no late. See you later. I love you my love. Every day, every way," grinning at me, he climbed into the Mitsubishi truck and drove off to the Air Force base in San Isidro, forty-five minutes away.

In the meantime I had worked out the salaries, some for the day and more for those who had worked all week. I took the little brown wages envelopes and wrote the names and amounts to be paid on each one.

The day continued as usual, I went on the computer, checking emails and playing spider solitaire. As noon approached there seemed to be a lot of noise outside the gate, and I went to investigate. There were several women standing outside, waiting for their menfolk to be paid and for them to hand over their wages. Also waiting was a lawyer, who had recently paid to get one of the workers out of jail for illegal arms possession, and wanted to recoup some of her outlay. As I was to find out later, she told him if he didn't start to pay her immediately, he was going back to jail.

Twelve o'clock arrived and no sign of Danilo. I called him on the phone.

"Danilo, where the hell are you? I need the money to pay the workers!" I exclaimed angrily down the telephone.

"I come later. I be there one o'clock," he replied brusquely, and hung up the phone. I went outside the gate and announced to the crowd, "Danilo is coming soon. In *una hora* he will be here." There was some disgruntled muttering and cross looking faces.

At one o'clock I called him again. "Danilo, they are waiting, you have to get home now!" "I can't, they called me to work. Tell them tomorrow they have money," he snapped, and once again cut the call. I was furious as I hated letting people down and went outside to talk with the men.

"Listen, I'm sorry, but Danilo is busy. Come tomorrow in the morning and I will give you the money," I said apologetically. There was considerably more muttering, but slowly they began to drift off in ones and twos.

By four o'clock Danilo was still not home and by now his telephone was switched off. I knew when he was working for the DNI his phone would have been removed and kept by the team leader. This was to stop members of the team from warning the drug dealers, or paedophiles, or arms dealers or whoever, that they were coming. If you warn criminals there is going to be a raid, apparently they give you a payoff for warning them. When Danilo's phone was off, invariably he had been called to work and I never knew when he would be home. There was always the possibility his phone had run out of charge or he had had an accident, and although I wasn't overly concerned, I did feel slightly uncomfortable. I was also cross he had not got back to pay the workers, as I knew they needed their money, but I knew he would not have had a choice.

The day passed peacefully enough and once dinner was over, I decided to go out to Freedom Bar where there was karaoke every Saturday night, and I could meet up with Margaret and have a chat with Sue. Danilo and I would go there every Saturday, although sometimes I would go alone if he was working. There was no one in the house when I left, as the children were at baseball camp in San Pedro de Macoris for the weekend. The only person around was Luis, the night watchman who lived in a little hut in the garden, to make sure no one stole any of the building materials while we were in the middle of construction.

Fancying a change of clothing, I dressed in clothes from a previous life, Armani jeans and a red Dolce and Gabbana

T-shirt, with a matching red leather clutch bag and set off in my jeep to the bar, five minutes drive away.

I arrived at the bar about a quarter to ten. It was already full and people were singing karaoke. I chatted and shook hands with friends as I went up to the bar.

"Hiya Margaret, hey Terry."

"Lindsay! How are you? You look great!" replied Margaret, in her southern American accent.

"I'm fine, but appear to have lost Danilo – for a change!" I smiled ruefully.

Terry got up from his bar stool and offered it to me and I smiled at him. "Thanks Terry," I said, hoisting myself onto the stool next to Margaret, and started chatting to her and Sue, running through the events of my day.

I would normally stay till the bar closed, usually one in the morning, but for some reason this particular evening I felt uncomfortable, restless. At ten twenty or so I decided to leave. Danilo was still not answering his phone, and I was not in the mood for karaoke.

"Listen Margaret, I'm going home," I said, jumping off my stool.

"No, stay a while, I want to sing with you," she pleaded.

"Hey, Lindsay, stay a while, it's early yet," said Terry. "I'll buy you another rum."

"Sorry, I'm just not in the mood tonight. I've no idea why, but I really want to go home. See you guys later!" I said goodbye to everyone, and although more asked me to stay, I drove off. I had no idea why, I just wanted to be at home.

A couple of minutes later I drove up the bumpy track and arrived at the house, parking as usual outside the gates, climbed out and locked the jeep. It was our habit to park the cars outside and bring them inside the gates before we went to bed. Or sometimes we would leave them on the track outside, as it was usually pretty safe.

There were two ways of getting into the garden. One was to roll the whole gate back, which we did to bring the cars inside, and the other was to enter by a small gate in the middle of the big gate. That was my normal way in, as the main gate was usually padlocked on the inside.

Two men were standing by the gate and it seemed they were trying to open it. They looked Haitian, one short and stocky, and the other tall, with his hair braided. They looked familiar and I realised the taller one had been working on the house that morning. I approached them and noticed the padlock on the ground, which I thought was odd.

There were often people outside the gate waiting to see Danilo, so it wasn't strange in itself, but I felt a little uneasy.

"*Buenas noches*," I said, and decided to continue opening the large gate, already open a few inches, and close it behind me before I told them Danilo was not yet home. They didn't answer me, but stood back a little to let me past. I slid the large gate open about two feet, went inside, and turned around. I had my hand on the gate to roll it shut, when the taller of the two men looked at the other as if he was about to ask a question. The stocky one simply nodded his head and said, "*Da le*," which means 'give it to her', or 'go for it'.

What the hell do they want to give me? I wondered. The next few seconds happened in a flash.

The taller of the two men lifted his T-shirt and pulled a gun from his trouser waistband. I was incredulous. *The man had a gun!*

Instinctively I knew I had to run and get away, but before I could move, he lifted his arm and fired. I saw a flash of light and heard a deafening noise before instinct took over and I ran to the back of the house, looking for somewhere to hide. I thought they would follow me, but hearing no sounds of pursuit, I crouched down and rifled frantically through my handbag looking for my phone.

Suddenly the dogs started barking crazily. *Oh no, please don't hurt my dogs*, I thought desperately, and ran to the corner of the house, peering round the wall, terrified and in shock, to see what was happening.

More shots and the dogs were going wild, jumping up at the men, snarling savagely and barking. I moved back to my hiding place and picked up the phone, but couldn't think straight. *Who shall I call? What should I do? Make a bloody decision woman!* I screamed to myself. The decision was made for me as I collapsed onto the rough concrete floor. My face felt peculiar, sort of numb, and I tasted blood in my mouth. My red top was soaking wet, and I had no idea why. I couldn't breathe. It was as if I was breathing in water. *Oh my God, I've been shot. But where? What should I do, what should I do?* I began to panic and suddenly from nowhere came an unexpected feeling of calm and peacefulness,

"Daaaaddddyyy!" I screamed out loud, "My daaddddy!" I was going to die, I knew it. "Mum, I'm sorry," I yelled. For some reason I had to talk and fast. "Danilo, I love you. I want more time, please give me more time."

I was gasping like a fish out of water with blood bubbling out of my mouth and nose. At the time I assumed I'd been shot in the back, probably as I ran away. I found out much later I had been shot in the throat before I turned and ran.

The bullet had entered my throat, gone through my right lung and was lodged in my back. The air from my punctured lung escaped into my face and chest cavity, which was filling with air and blood, while the other lung was slowly collapsing. As my face and neck swelled up, my necklace cut into me, and my eyes were slowly closing. Not only were my lungs collapsing, my windpipe was getting smaller and smaller under the pressure of the air and the blood. I have only hazy recollections of what happened after that; what follows is a combination of information given to me by the people who were there and memories of my own, as I faded in and out of awareness.

In the meantime, unbeknown to me, Jason and Juander had returned to the house and were cooking plantains and salami in the kitchen. Jason was staying with us, and Juander was a Dominican working on the construction of the kids' house and also living with us. As the pair were cooking salami, the four dogs were also in the kitchen hoping for scraps rather than waiting for me at the gate – Fred, Tyson, the Great Dane, and their five month old puppies, Sophie and *el Mas Guapo*, the 'fiercest' or 'angriest', as he would growl at anything. Can Can had died of cancer a few months earlier.

Hearing the shots, Juander immediately turned to Jason and screamed, "Go get the shotgun from under the bed!" and ran outside. By the time he got to the front of the house, the men had gone and the dogs were still barking and hurling themselves at the gate. Juander was scared to approach, but slowly moved towards the dogs, scanning around as he moved nervously towards them. He spotted my parked jeep outside.

"Jason, where is Lindsay?" he yelled. "Jason, where the hell are you?" Juander ran back to the house and found Jason hiding under the bed with the shotgun.

"Get out you stupid idiot, we have to find the *jefa*!" and he ran into the bathroom to the toilet. He stood there, having a pee, and he heard me shout for my dad at the back of the house.

"Jason, she's here, quickly!" he yelled, and ran around to the back. I was aware of Juander standing over me and screaming, "Lindsay's dead! Lindsay's dead!"

I squinted up at him. "Not dead," I gasped thickly, fighting to breathe, struggling to get every word out through the blood still foaming through my nose and mouth. "Hospital... hospital... hospital."

Juander was unable to think, terrified and shocked. I tried to tell him to take me to Dr Galvas, who had a private clinic only a few minutes drive away. He seemed more concerned about taking off my jewellery. First my necklace, then he started pulling at my rings and watch. I had no idea why, but found out afterwards the police have a habit of stealing jewellery from dead bodies.

Juander carried me out into the dusty street, where a large crowd of Haitians had gathered after hearing the gunshots and the dogs going wild. Angelita was among them and managed to take my handbag. Everyone was screaming and yelling, "Lindsay dead! Lindsay dead!" The noise was deafening. In the end they put me in my jeep, in the passenger seat, and six or seven people squeezed in the back. Juander sat in the driver's seat.

"Oh shit, I can't drive!" he screamed.

"I will!" yelled someone from the back. Reconfiguration took place as he climbed into the back and someone else climbed into the front. The new driver tried to start the car, but the jeep was not an automatic and none of them knew how to drive it. You have to depress the clutch before you can start the ignition. I tried to tell them but my brain and mouth weren't functioning and the words wouldn't come out.

"Lindsay drive!" someone shouted manically, and everyone scrambled out and put me in the driver's seat. I couldn't see as my eyes had swollen shut and I was having difficulty breathing, nor did I seem to be able to think clearly. Realising this wasn't going to work, everyone got out of the car and laid me down on the dirt road.

"*Hopital*," I whispered faintly, wheezing with every gasp, "*Por favor, hopital*. Carry me, carry me, please hospital." Juander and another Haitian scooped me up and carried me, running along the track with forty or more Haitians behind, yelling and screaming I was dead. Halfway to the clinic a *motoconcho* stopped to help and I was unceremoniously draped over the back of his bike. A few minutes later we arrived at the doctor's surgery.

I thought once I got there everything would be alright. It was not to be.

Jason had meanwhile come out from under the bed and was running round like a headless chicken. He tried to call 911 and there was no reply. He called the police station, but the phone had been cut off as the bill had not been paid. He called Billy, the manager of the *colmado* who I worked with at the dive school, and who had just climbed into bed. Billy threw on his clothes, ran outside and jumped on his motorbike, but, too frightened to come on his own, went to Vic and Rachel, an English couple from Leeds, who had recently become our partners in the *colmado*. Billy blew his horn and screamed outside their house, "Lindsay's been shot!"

Rachel ran to the door and peered out. "Billy? What the hell do you want?"

"Hurry, Lindsay's been shot! We have to do something!"

"Vic!" she yelled. "Come quick, Billy says Lindsay's been shot!" Vic threw on a T-shirt, ran outside and together they rode to the clinic where I had just arrived on the back of the *motoconcho*.

The door to the clinic was firmly closed. It seemed everyone was banging on the door and yelling. "Doctor, open the door, Lindsay's been shot!" they screamed, hammering on the glass with their fists. A nurse came to the door and opened it a fraction.

"Sorry, we are closed," she announced calmly, and moved to close the door. They shoved past her forcing their way in. Vic carried me inside and lay me down on the bed in the consulting room.

"Do something for her!" he demanded, with an air of authority. The doctor appeared from the back of the clinic pulling on his white coat and looked down at me.

"Nothing can be done," he pronounced calmly. "No one can survive this. She might still be breathing now, but not for much longer. She will be dead shortly. Leave her here if you want, and tell her husband to come and collect the body when he returns. I will call the coroner now to certify death, as she will be dead by the time he gets here. Now you can all leave."

"No way!" yelled Billy. "We can't leave her! We must do *something*. We need a car!" He ran out into the street, desperately looking for a car to flag down. Meanwhile, Angelita decided to become the town crier and went down to Freedom Bar on the same bike, which had taken me to the clinic. She ran into the middle of the packed bar screaming, "Lindsay is dead!"

Chaos followed her announcement. I had been there chatting only twenty minutes before, although it seemed like hours ago. Margaret and Terry didn't think twice and ran outside, flung themselves into their car and drove to Dr Galvas' clinic.

At the same time, Chi Chi, the *maestro*, had been woken up at his house by someone yelling I was dead, and while running to my house was picked up by a Haitian in a jeep, and together they raced to the clinic. Billy saw them arriving.

"Thank goodness, quickly they won't help her here! We need to go to San Pedro. Now!" Chi Chi bundled me into the jeep and he, Billy, Juander and I set off for San Pedro de Macoris, closely followed by Margaret and Terry in their car.

The drive to San Pedro was chaotic. The Haitian driver was terrified and nearly had several accidents. I lay across Billy and Chi Chi in the back seat. By now I couldn't feel or see anything, but I could hear Billy. He spoke to me in near perfect English. "Please don't die, Lindsay, don't die! Hold on, we're nearly there. Don't die. Don't die. Just a few minutes more. Hold on."

I fought to respond with only one word, "Danilo. I want Danilo."

We arrived at the first clinic in San Pedro. I was carried inside and laid across a line of plastic chairs in the waiting room. The doctor on duty called a few people in the hospital, said they were unable to help and turned us away. He told the guys I needed a tracheotomy, which they could not perform there, as they did not have the equipment.

Luckily, to save driving to every hospital in San Pedro to try and find one which did have the right equipment, Chi Chi had the presence of mind to ask him to telephone and see which hospital could help. Finally they found one. Meanwhile the doctor had called the police and when we arrived at the second clinic there was a reception committee of a colonel, two captains and a host of policemen.

This was not a welcome sight to the men who were with me in the car. Before we got out of the car they quickly turned their T-shirts inside out to hide my blood, as they would have been arrested for questioning if they were thought to be involved. I was carried inside and laid on a trolley, where the police came over to look at me and seemed most upset I had no jewellery. The doctors were waiting, but before they would do anything they asked who was going to pay. Chi Chi told them I was rich and that I, or my husband, would pay and not to worry about the money.

Once the financial discussions were over they wheeled me along the corridor, carried me up two flights of stairs and into a small room where the doctors performed a tracheotomy. A life saving measure they told me afterwards. Unfortunately, they cut straight through my vocal chords as they performed the procedure in the wrong place. We are not talking about a beautiful, plastic, state of the art tracheotomy tube. It was an old metal thing tied around my neck by a piece of dirty bandage. Nor was it a tiny little hole, it was a four-inch long slash.

Whilst I was having my throat cut, with no anaesthetic, the crowd gathering downstairs included Margaret and Terry, and the police were interviewing the guys who bought me in the car. More and more people were arriving on motorbikes from Juan Dolio. The waiting room was crowded and slowly the car park began to fill with people too.

Margaret was allowed to come and see me once they had done the tracheotomy. She kept asking who had done this, but I was unable to speak. She said afterwards my arms were flailing and I was kicking my feet, and obviously having problems breathing. I knew I was drowning and finding it hard to breathe. In my mind I was diving underwater and desperately kicking my fins to reach the surface for air, but, hard as I tried, I couldn't get there. My face and clothes were covered with blood and I kept pointing to my wedding ring. *Where the hell was Danilo?*

Danilo and his fellow DNI members were in La Romana, a town forty minutes to the east of San Pedro, having just finished their night's work. They were sitting down to a meal of salami and plantains when they were given their phones back. Danilo switched his on and was shocked at the number of messages. Suddenly it rang again and for the first time since lunchtime, he answered. It was Billy.

"Danilo, Lindsay's been shot! She is going to die! Get here now. Now!" He didn't bother finishing his dinner and together with a posse of police and DNI officers, Army and Air Force, they came charging back from La Romana to San Pedro. On the way he listened to his messages with most telling him I was dead. He decided to call me to see if it was true. Angelita took the call as she had my handbag with my phone in it. (The bag and the phone made it back to me, but the money inside never did.) She told him I had been taken to San Pedro and he arrived at the hospital running in to see me. As the doctors were performing the tracheotomy, he was told to leave and only allowed in when it was over. I was unaware of all the emotion. The doctors were pretty sure I wouldn't make it, they said it would take a miracle for me to survive. People were crying, including Danilo, and some were scared they would be arrested. Margaret and Terry went out into the car park and prayed.

Apart from being genuinely concerned about my well being, the Dominicans and Haitians who had helped me were terrified I would die. If I died without anyone knowing who had shot me, then Danilo and the children would have been arrested and Danilo would have been charged with murder. Usually in the DR if a woman is shot, it is her husband who is responsible. Everyone who had helped me would have been jailed, in case they were involved. They all had very good reasons for wanting me to make it through this and things were not looking good.

The tracheotomy was not helping. I still couldn't breathe, so they began to bag me with oxygen. It was decided I needed chest drains and they were not available anywhere in San Pedro. The doctors told Danilo the only way of saving my life was to take me to Plaza de la Salud hospital in the capital, an hour's drive away. The hunt was on for an ambulance, but none were to be found. After an endless wait, one of the DNI men found one belonging to the local Red Cross, but first we had to pay to fill it with diesel. The windscreen was badly cracked, the tyres were bald, it had no lights, and it was tiny and very hot inside. It was all there was. Margaret and Terry offered to take me in their car, but the doctor insisted on an ambulance. Possibly something to do with her commission payment from the ambulance driver.

They carried me down the stairs and into the ambulance, together with Danilo and a doctor. The doctor continued to bag me with oxygen and Danilo was trying to stop me from pulling the tracheotomy out. It was stiflingly hot in the tiny ambulance, as I rolled from side to side with the ambulance driver going as fast as he could.

"Nearly there," commented the doctor, peering out of the little cracked window. He looked at the oxygen bottle.

"Shit, it's finished!" he exclaimed.

"What the hell do you mean, finished?" yelled Danilo, frantically. "Do something, for God's sake."

The doctor took the bag out of the tracheotomy and stared down at me. Without the bag I could not breathe by myself. I felt myself beginning to shut down and frantically slashed my hand across my throat, the diving signal for out of air. With my other hand I waved goodbye to Danilo. I heard him sobbing loudly, the last thing I heard before losing consciousness again.

The ambulance turned into Plaza de la Salud, a state of the art hospital in Santo Domingo, where they were waiting for me. It was 3.40 in the morning and five hours since I had been shot. They rushed me into the ER but Danilo had to pay the ambulance and the doctor who had come with us. Luckily he still had the money he had taken out of the bank to pay the workers. They would not admit me to the ER without a deposit. A cash machine was next to the ER for such emergencies and he was able to withdraw more money to pay them. The financial business over, everyone was told to wait outside and they took me into the ER, where they worked on me for three hours and put in chest drains.

My God, they are a brilliant invention. Suddenly I could breathe on my own and open my eyes and for the first time since I had been carried up the road by Juander, I was fully aware of my surroundings and what was going on. My brain started to work again. I was still full of air in the top half of my body and had the biggest boobs I ever had in my life. If you pressed my arms they squeaked. They tried to take off my wedding ring, and won, though I fought them, but worst of all they cut off my Dolce and Gabbana top. My jeans had disappeared somewhere along the way, although why you have to take off jeans for a throat injury I have no idea.

I heard them asking Danilo for information. He managed my name and address but had no idea of my blood group, and he said they were not to give me blood. He was not convinced the blood would have been checked for AIDS or Hepatitis or anything else. When asked my age he said thirty-seven, and in my befuddled state I tried desperately to tell the doctors I was actually fifty. I wished he had listened to me before when I had tried to tell him my real age

They sat me up to take an x-ray (none of those posh ones on the ceiling) where they saw the bullet lodged close to my spine. I thought they would operate to take it out, but they decided to leave it where it was. When they sat me up I shook the doctors' hands and gasped, "Thank you," remembering my Dominican manners. And at last the head surgeon, Dr Hussein, went outside and gave the crowd in the car park the news they had anxiously been waiting for.

"She is out of danger!"

A massive cheer went up from the car park, and the ER filled as everyone came in to see me. I was full of tubes. Two chest drains, each leading into a demi-john with water in on the floor, a catheter, and drips in both arms containing goodness knows what. I didn't have any painkillers and now, for the first time I felt pain. And what pain. I felt like had been run over by a bus. My whole chest, which was gradually turning black from neck to my waist, hurt. Danilo and the police came in.

"Lindsay, what hatping? Who do this?" Danilo asked. I started to try and speak but Dr Hussein yelled, "Don't talk! You have a tracheotomy, you shouldn't speak!" The three policemen bent closer. I signalled two with my hand. "Haitian or Dominican?" demanded the police.

"Haitian," I mouthed. I wanted to tell them about the braids and gestured I wanted a pen and paper and wrote it down. *There were two men, one tall and one short, the tall one had braids. Was building house.* The fact one had braids ensured great business for the barbers in Juan Dolio as the word went out from the police and every male in the area who had braids was arrested. There were massive queues at the barbers as they rushed to cut them off. A few days later it became apparent the man who shot me was the one I had recognised, who had been working on the new roof for the guesthouse and whose lawyer had been waiting for him outside the gate. He needed money to pay off his lawyer or he would go back to jail. I had told the workers earlier in the day they would be paid on Sunday, and he assumed the money for all of the workers would be in the house that night.

Back in Juan Dolio, the police arrived at the house and put Jason under house arrest. They checked the house and started searching the garden for shells. In all they recovered four shells and two bullets. One bullet was in my back and the other bullet was in one of the dogs – *el Mas Guapo*. I knew a dog had been shot, and kept telling Danilo, but he assured me they were all fine. And, indeed he did seem fine at the time.

Jason was questioned repeatedly. The police seemed interested in the relationship between Danilo and I, if we argued or fought. Should I die, they would arrest Danilo and the police would take the house. This was standard procedure for people who were arrested. After leaving prison they would find everything they owned had been taken. Whilst most people were hoping for my survival, the local police were not among them.

Juander returned from the hospital in San Pedro and was not allowed past the gates into the house and garden. Other friends and the children, who had been in baseball camp in San Pedro, arrived and were told to stay outside. They stayed there all night, together with Luis the *watchyman*, who made it out from under his bed where he had hidden as soon as he heard the shots, barricaded in with a few sacks of cement. Everyone was interviewed at length.

When they took me to a room, at 7.30am in the morning, I was in a lot of pain and asked for painkillers. Unfortunately, they were not allowed to give strong painkillers on a Sunday. More people started to arrive, police, members of the government, DNI staff, English friends, Danilo's family, and Compres and José Luis Bencosme. An armed guard was placed outside the door of my room. Police photographers came and took pictures of me. I felt like a film star though I looked like the Michelin man.

In the Dominican Republic, friends and family rally round when you are dead, in jail, or in hospital. In all, over four hundred people came to see me and I was never alone, day or night for the twelve days I was there. Danilo was with me twenty-four hours a day and for the first few days would sleep on a chair next to the bed, holding my hand so I could squeeze if I needed anything.

I was still finding it hard to breathe, couldn't speak, and every time I coughed, which was every few minutes or so, the tracheotomy tube flew across the room and someone had to put it back in, having cleaned off the dust and fluff. No one was keen on this job and I would gasp like a fish until it was back in.

Although off the critical list, I was still seriously ill. Rachel came in later the same day and I was so pleased to see her, along with Sue, Terry and Margaret.

"Please, it hurts," I whispered. "It hurts so much, and they won't give me anything. Please can you make them give me something for this pain." Rachel marched out and I could hear her shouting at the nurses in Spanish, with a British northern twang. She came back in and sat down next to the bed on a plastic chair, and pushed her dark shiny bob behind her ears.

"Right, that's them sorted. They'll bring you something for the pain now. I said morphine – is that alright?" I smiled gratefully and nodded. "Lindsay we have to tell your mother," she went on. I nodded, and stretched out my hand for a piece of paper and a pen.

Please don't upset her. I spoke to her yesterday. Wait a bit. I wrote.

"No, we shouldn't wait," she replied. "She needs to know. What if you get worse?" I wrote furiously, *No. Best call sister. Elisabeth can tell her.*

Rachel took my phone from Danilo, found the number, and went outside to make the call. I knew Elisabeth wasn't the sort to panic and having been a nurse she would understand the situation better. She could have the unenviable job of calling my mother.

Rachel also called the British embassy, thinking they might help in some way. Unfortunately the embassy was between ambassadors and unable to help, saying that as I was married to a Dominican I was not considered to be a British citizen. This turned out to be incorrect, as I had not taken Dominican citizenship. They did, however, ask for the telephone number of my mother and said they would inform her if I died.

I didn't cry throughout any of this, even though the pain was almost unbearable, not until my mother called a few hours later. "Are you alright?" she asked.

"Yes, I'm fine," I rasped quietly.

"You know there's no point in my coming now as I don't speak Spanish, but I will come once you get out of hospital. Of course, if your father were alive he would have come straight away." That did it. Talking about Dad, I sat sobbing uncontrollably for a while.

I was finding it very hard to speak and had hardly any voice, only a hoarse whisper. The police interviews continued, and they told me to tell everyone I had no idea who had shot me.

Given the speed of the jungle drums, the perpetrators soon heard I hadn't recognised them and returned to their little hut (*casita*) about 800 yards behind my house. As soon as they returned they were arrested.

Day by day I improved, but I was hungry, starving, and the doctors wouldn't let me eat. I would beg them to let me have something to eat or drink but they would refuse – they said they had no idea what damage had been done to my throat. After a couple of days I got out of bed. I was determined to get home as fast as possible, as I knew every day was costing money. Luckily we had medical insurance and the insurance company came in most days to see how I was doing. I kept asking if they would pay everything and they just smiled and said, "We'll see."

Klaus came to see me and insisted I be moved to a private room and he would pay the difference in costs. Whilst very generous of him, this turned out to be a bad move. I was duly moved, but not only was the room more expensive, so was everything else, the bandages, the drugs, the x-rays, the doctor's time, everything. My insurance would have covered everything in the standard room, but not if I was in the private area. The bill when we left was enormous, over £15,000. As the insurance company were unable to split the difference between the costs of the standard and private room I ended up paying for it, apart from the insurance company contribution which was about half.

The nurses in Dominican hospitals are not like British nurses. They only give you injections, and change drips. My friends, Danilo and his family washed me, washed my hair, and were in charge of bedpans once the catheter was out. After about a week I would try to go to the bathroom, carrying all my various bottles and tubes. The first time I stood up, there was blood on the floor. Danilo panicked. I realised I had started my period, as I had not been taking my HRT pills. He was duly dispatched to find a sanitary towel, which he did and put it on. On my next visit to the toilet, being helped by Sue and Rachel, we discovered he had put it on upside down. In order to take it off, I had to give myself a Brazilian wax and the three of us had hysterics realising what he had done

Every other day I had a chest x-ray to see if my lungs had re-inflated. Eventually they took out one chest drain and finally, at last, the other. I still hadn't had anything to eat or drink and was weak and very hungry. I would beg Dr Hussein to let me eat every time he came to see me. Once the last drain was out I was free to go. My friends did not want me to go back to the house and all offered their homes for me to stay in. But I was determined to return home. And so, twelve days after I was shot, I came home.

I wanted to walk out to the car park but was too dizzy, instead I was wheeled down in a wheelchair. Danilo obviously had to drive, which was a nerve-racking experience, but finally we reached Juan Dolio and as we passed the Freedom Bar I asked him to stop. I walked into the bar shakily, slowly and carefully putting one foot in front of the other, leaning on Danilo and my stomach welcomed its first nourishment since I had been shot. Another shot, this time of *Brugal* rum. Everyone was delighted to see me and within minutes the word was out on the street.

We returned to the house, which had been decorated with balloons and signs saying, *Welcome Home!* Unfortunately, every time a balloon burst I nearly had a heart attack, thinking it was a gunshot.

The dogs were ecstatic to see me. They all ran up to me, apart from *el Mas Guapo*. I walked over to him and bent down.

He wagged his tail, looked up and laid his head on his front paws and died. He had been shot in the bottom and no one had known, as the bullet hole was small. I was heartbroken, as had someone found the bullet hole they may have been able to save his life.

I had survived and was left with a profound gratitude to those people who helped me. They did so selflessly, knowing there was a good chance they would be arrested. Without them I would have died. I was also very grateful to those who came to visit me in hospital and when I came out. The generosity of spirit of the Dominican and Haitian people really did come shining through. Some went to Higuey, a city some two hours away, to light candles to the Virgin Mary at the cathedral and prayed I might live. The inefficiency of the health system, the lack of ambulances and nationwide emergency medicine, made me appreciate the British health service. The fact it is limited in the DR means your friends and family become much more important.

The experience marked a turning point for me as to how I saw the country and its people. I realised the important things in life were not what possessions you had, or what you had in your fridge, or if there was a scratch on the car. What was important was being there for your fellow man, and helping when you could. If they were hungry, feed them, desperate for money, help them out.

But I could no longer dive, I could no longer sing, and I could hardly speak. Yet my relationship with Danilo deepened, and his with me. He had come close to losing me, he realised how important I was to him, and the fact he had looked after me so well made me realise how very much I loved him too.

THERE ARE FOUR TYPES OF HOSPITAL IN THE DOMINICAN REPUBLIC. The first is the public hospital. There is one in every reasonable sized town and the medical treatment is free, but all medicines and x-rays, stitches etc. have to be paid for. The standard of care is average at best and although they are the norm for most Dominicans, they should only be used in dire emergencies. The in-patient is expected to provide their own sheets, pillows, toilet paper, food etc, and they are looked after by members of their family.

The second type of hospitals are the major world-class hospitals available in the capital, Santo Domingo, and Santiago. These hospitals have the latest equipment and top medical professionals. They have private facilities, but even the public facilities are two-bedded rooms with bathroom. The health care is not free and payment is made for the room and the medical help. All take insurance though. These hospitals will undertake all medical procedures including organ transplants.

The third type are the high quality hospitals and clinics in the tourist areas. Whilst not as large as the major hospitals in Santo Domingo or Santiago, these are high quality clinics with a high standard of in-patient care and all doctors and staff speak English. Finally there are the local clinics, used by the local people. There are usually 3 to 5 in each town. They will generally be a higher standard than the public hospital, but not as high as those in tourist areas. There are single in-patient rooms with bathrooms and televisions, and are fine for basic operations or broken bones – anything more complex will need to be referred to a larger hospital. Costs are significantly lower than the tourist clinics or the major hospitals.

All Dominican hospitals put patients on a saline drip immediately, and will also almost always administer IV antibiotics, whatever the problem. The nursing staff do not perform the same duties as in the UK and USA – they only administer injections, change dressings etc. The family is supposed to look after the patient, bathe them and provide food, and most family members will stay with the patient around the clock.

Ambulances are hard to come by, and although there is 911 as an emergency number, it rarely works. Most emergencies are taken to hospital by friends or in the back of a police pick up.

WHAT ABOUT YOUR SAUCEPANS?

CHAPTER SIX
BACK TO NORMAL

ONCE I RETURNED HOME LIFE SLOWLY RETURNED TO NORMAL. Mum came out to stay for two weeks and was a great help as I was still in a lot of pain, particularly where the chest drains had been. One morning, in the early sunshine, we sat out on the patio drinking our coffee.

"I wonder why I didn't die?" I thought out loud.

"Maybe it wasn't your time," she replied, taking a sip from her mug.

"Chi Chi said it was because I'd had a glass of rum and my blood was warm," I said giggling. "And others say I'm being saved to do something special."

"That sounds nice," replied Mum.

"Yes, I just wish I knew what it was. I feel fine, I don't have nightmares or anything, I just want to know why I'm not dead," I persevered.

"I wouldn't be surprised if your dad had something to do with you surviving, but I think it's called survivor guilt," Mum answered. "People get it if they survive a car crash and others don't. Anyway let's get your wounds washed for the day."

We got up and went into the bathroom. I still had two large holes under my armpits where the chest drains went in, which were stitched but needed cleaning twice a day, and I had stitches in the gash across my neck.

I went back to Plaza de la Salud hospital twice, once to have the stitches out and once to have the bullet removed. The bullet was very near to the surface of my back and therefore uncomfortable to lie down – I felt like the princess with the pea under the mattress – and it was taken out with a Gillette razor blade. I wanted to wear it on a chain around my neck, but the police took it away as evidence.

Mum and I became a lot closer during this time. It was her first visit without Dad, and it gave us two weeks together to sit and talk. When she left I missed her and from then on we would Skype each other every day, whereas before we would talk maybe once a week. She wanted me to go back to England with her, but I did not want to leave. My home was in the Dominican Republic with Danilo.

Not long after I came out of hospital I became aware of rumours. For some reason people seemed unable to comprehend or accept I had been shot during an attempted burglary. The two men responsible for shooting me had been arrested and admitted they had shot me, as they had assumed all the wages money was in the house. Although Danilo had the money on him when he was called to go to work, it had all been spent on the doctor in San Pedro and the ambulance.

Danilo and I knew why it had happened but the local expats, maybe to make themselves feel safer, began to make up stories. One morning I wandered into Freedom Bar for a coffee and perched on a barstool. There was an expat sitting next to me.

"Hi," she said in an American accent.

"Good morning," I replied politely.

"You're the girl who got shot, aren't you?" she went on. "Do they know who did it yet?"

"Yes." I replied curtly, not wanting to get into a conversation with someone I didn't know. She didn't take the hint.

"I heard they wore masks," she continued.

"Really, and where did you hear that?" I asked incredulously, sipping my coffee.

"Oh round and about," she said, waving her hands in the air.

"Well, they didn't. I was there, I know what happened, I know who they are, and they are in jail." With that I left abruptly, as I didn't want to hear more rubbish. I drove off to another bar, and again, as soon as people saw me walking in I was aware of whispers and stares, and felt distinctly uncomfortable.

Danilo was hearing the rumours too. They varied from a drug deal gone wrong, to him arranging to have me shot. He and I both became more and more upset and having been happy to come home, I couldn't understand why everyone had to gossip and speculate on what was a straightforward robbery.

Rachel, who had been a great support when I was in hospital, came over to the house one morning for coffee. "Hi, Linds, how are you feeling?" she asked.

"Not too bad, each day I feel a little better, thanks." We sat down on the patio, looking out into the garden.

"I was in San Pedro yesterday," she said, haltingly.

"Really?" I asked, knowing she wanted to tell me something.

"Yes, and I ran into that Canadian girl, you know, the fat one who was going out with one of the guys who shot you?"

"Oh right, silly cow she is. He used to beat her up didn't he?"

"Yes, that's the one. Anyway she said Danilo had arranged to have you shot, and it was Saya who did it."

"Stupid bitch," I muttered angrily. "Don't you think I would known if it was Saya. I know who it was and they are in jail. I have no idea why no one believes me. Anyway, why would Danilo want to shoot me? He would have everything to lose and nothing to gain. We never even argue for God's sake."

The rumours and the gossip didn't stop. Slowly I stopped going out as much as every time I went into a bar or restaurant, I couldn't help but notice the stares followed by hushed and furtive conversations and more stares. The Canadian woman paid $1,000 US for her boyfriend to be released, and he and his brother were let out of jail and back on the streets. I was very concerned they would come and find me and shoot me, to stop me testifying in the future if they were ever arrested again, however it appeared they had moved out of the area.

But they hadn't moved far as two months later they robbed and beat a 75-year-old Canadian man to death with a baseball bat. He lived just around the corner from us. One was arrested again, and the other disappeared. The one arrested was sentenced to 30 years in jail. A year later his sister paid for his release. In the end he was arrested for another murder, and as far as I am aware he's still in jail.

The fact I was unable to speak very well was incredibly annoying. Danilo bought me a whistle, which I would wear round my neck, as I couldn't shout, and everyone was given a number of peeps. Danilo was one, Dany two etcetera. I discovered I could speak on a one to one basis, but if there was any noise, such as a fan, or music in a car, or other people talking, I couldn't be heard. Another reason not to go out, and whilst our nights at bars and dancing didn't come to a total standstill, we went out far less often. The days of euphoria had come to an abrupt end and life moved into a different phase.

There was no Victim Support in the DR, no psychiatrists came to visit, and, although I was fine, I felt a need to talk to someone about what happened, but the expats who I thought were my friends were slowly becoming less important. Apart from the rumours, I began to see them in a different light.

I had befriended a Haitian woman who was having twins. Unfortunately, one twin died at birth and the other a couple of months later. I was telling a supposed expat friend about this.

"I feel sorry for her, she was so looking forward to the babies," I related. "How can someone get over the death of two children like that?"

"Well," she replied knowledgeably, "it won't be too bad for her, *they* don't think like we do, so it's no big deal. *They* don't have proper feelings." My mouth dropped open in shock.

"What did you just say?" I asked, incredulously.

"No need to look like that," she snapped. "You know it's true. Listen, the Dominicans and Haitians just aren't like us. They're mostly retards."

I couldn't believe what I was hearing and I realised I didn't want to spend my time with people who could say such insensitive and offensive things. Maybe her real feelings towards the locals had been there before and I hadn't been aware of it. I was married to a Dominican, I had Dominican stepsons and I did not want to mix with people who were disparaging, insulting and offensive. I had always thought I could live in two camps, have a Dominican life and an expat life, but it was becoming apparent this was not going to be possible when some expats had attitudes like this.

As we were going out less I started to spend more time on the Internet, and discovered a forum for the Dominican Republic called DR1.com. I posted about the shooting and it was the beginning of a series of friendships, which would see me through the years to come. The people I became closest to were all fellow Brits who lived on the north coast of the island. Shirley, who lived with her partner, Charlie, in a beautiful *finca*, John who lived in Sosua and had an amazing sense of humour, and Ginnie, who lived in Puerto Plata, had been here for years and knew a great deal about the country and its people. The forum had a chat room and often at night the four of us would be chatting about what had happened during the day with typical British humour.

Slowly the gossip machine started to get weary of talking about us, and although we didn't go out as much, life carried on the same as before. We had a new gardener, Jean, who was Haitian. He was Jason's father-in-law and had arrived from Haiti the previous year. He was 60 years old, and, unable to find work locally, was spending all day in the *colmado*, cleaning and generally hanging around. As *Araña* had departed, we needed a new gardener and I was keen to have someone living in. Since being shot I had been a little nervous when I was on my own at night, which happened a couple of times a week when Danilo was working the night shift. The children's house had been finished and they were living in it, but if anything happened I could not shout for them as my voice was not strong enough.

Jean arrived and moved in. He spoke no Spanish, or English or French, only Creole. He was tall, long limbed and strong, but so thin you could see all his bones. I took him round the garden trying to explain what needed doing in a mixture of Creole and French and to everything I said he replied, "*Oui Oui*". From then on everyone called him Oui Oui. I showed him his *watchyman* house with a bed, a television, which had satellite programmes, and a little bathroom and living area.

"What do you think of it Oui Oui?" I asked in French.

"Good, good, very good," he replied beaming. The next day I bought him a two-ring gas cooker and a small fridge.

"Here you go, this is for you. You can eat with us at noon and in the night, but you can use this when we aren't here, or to make coffee in the morning, or whatever." He looked at me incredulously and broke down.

"In all my life I never had a fridge. This is first time," he grabbed hold of me and hugged me, tears running down his leathery face. He was paid the standard wage for a gardener of 5000 pesos a month, which is about £100. He had no fixed hours. I wanted him to make sure the garden was always tidy, and the pool clean but I didn't mind how long it took him. He soon got into a routine of getting up at five o'clock and sweeping up the leaves. He would then spend his day at the house with some time at the *colmado*. At six o'clock on the dot he would come and sit on the patio and drink a bottle of beer. I bought him a six-pack a week, and there he would sit, smiling, looking out at the garden waiting for dinner. After dinner we would all play dominos for an hour or two. He was a mean domino player and a dreadful cheat. He did a good job on the whole and the garden started to look lovely. However, if a tree shed too many leaves he would cut the tree down to make his life easier, and he created havoc with his machete. He seemed to have no idea how to prune anything and massacred trees and shrubs. Very quickly he became an established member of the family.

"Lindsay I have to go to dentist," he said to me one Sunday.

"Where is the dentist?" I asked.

"He is in the church. He is the pastor. He is pastor and dentist." There was a little Haitian church, constructed out of wood and plastic sheeting, down the road from us, and the pastor would hold his surgery after the church service. Oui Oui was missing his two front teeth so I assumed it may be about those. Off he trotted and returned an hour later holding a bloody handkerchief to his mouth.

"My God," I exclaimed. "What has he done?"

"He took out four teeth, and next week he take out four more, and then more, till I have no teeth," he explained.

"Why on earth are you having all of your teeth out?" I asked incredulously.

"Because I missed my front teeth, and he will get me a whole set of teeth."

All he wanted was to have his missing two front teeth replaced, and the only way to achieve that was to have all of his teeth removed and replaced with dentures. His dentures arrived but they were not made for him. He'd had to wait for someone to die who had dentures and then they were given to him. They didn't fit terribly well and to begin with every time he spoke they jiggled up and down, but in time he seemed to get used to them and they more or less stayed in place.

That Christmas we decided to go to England. The whole family, the two boys, Danilo and I. It was to be the boys' first visit to England and they were beside themselves with excitement. There were various reasons for going.

Firstly to spend Christmas with my mother. It was the second Christmas since my father died, and she did not want to go away, nor did she want to spend it alone. Secondly,

I wanted to have our marriage blessed in an English church with my family present, as none of them had been able to come to our wedding in the DR. I especially wanted my 99-year-old grandmother there. I had not spoken to her since I had been shot, as my voice was not strong enough for the telephone, and she was a little deaf. Worse, no one in the family had told her I had been shot, as they did not want to upset her. I wanted to see her, as before the shooting we'd spoken every week, and I knew she would be wondering why she had not heard from me for so long. And finally it would be lovely for the boys to go on a plane for the first time and to see England.

The boys nearly didn't make it. Around six weeks before we left, in early November, Danilo and I had been out, came home and were getting into bed when the phone rang.

"*Hola*," I said, as I picked it up.

"Put Danilo on," said the dwendy Saya at the other end.

"Not now, Saya. It's late and we are just going to bed. Talk to him in the morning." I replied, tersely.

"Put him on now!" he shouted. "It's important."

"Hold your bloody horses," I mumbled, as I yelled Danilo to come to the phone, and I went into the bathroom. I wasn't really listening, then Danilo barged into the bathroom.

"Come on, we have to go! Boys in accident."

"What do you mean, accident? Aren't they asleep in the guest house?" I asked, confused.

"No, they take my motorcycle! They in accident. They in hospital." We left quickly, driving to a private clinic in San Pedro and rushed inside. The boys were lying in a cubicle.

Dany had no skin on half of his face, his jeans and T-shirt were ripped and swathes of skin were missing with what looked like half the road embedded in his stomach. His knees were red raw and bleeding and there was blood coming out of the side of his head. Alberto was a little better as he had on two pairs of jeans. He thought his legs looked too thin so he always wore two pairs. He too had skin missing from his face, both of his arms and his stomach. He burst into tears when he saw me.

"I'm sorry Lindsay," he sobbed, "I'm sorry."

"Don't worry," I soothed him, stroking his matted and sticky head. "At least you're both alive with no bones broken."

Having seen they were alright, we discovered they had 'borrowed' Danilo's pride and joy, a yellow 1000 cc Ninja motorbike to go to a party in San Pedro. Dany had drunk rum for the first time in his life and driven back at 220 kilometres an hour, with Alberto on the back of the bike screaming at him to stop, begging him to slow down. When they came to the flyover over the motorway, faced with a sharp curve, Alberto, realising they would crash, had thrown himself off and gone skidding and sliding down the road. Dany was unable to make the turn and the bike had gone straight into the guardrail. Dany had fallen off and the bike flew through the air, over the guardrail and into the ravine below. Danilo was speechless with fury and marched out to go and find his beloved bike, while I spent the night with the boys in the hospital. The bike was beyond repair, and the children slowly healed but still bear the scars to this day.

A few days later Danilo turned to me. "I need to go and see *brujo*." A *brujo* is a witchdoctor.

"What on earth for?" I asked, incredulously.

"Because someone has spelled us. You shot, boys accident. I need cancel spell." And off he went to see the *brujo*, who confirmed we had indeed been the victim of witchcraft from someone who was jealous of Danilo.

He was unable to give the name of the person, but Danilo had to pay him some money and buy a whole range of items to take back to the *brujo* to cancel the spell. The items included a bottle of rum, black candles, oil and various lotions and potions from the local voodoo stall in the market. We washed with some foul smelling soap and covered ourselves with lotion, and Danilo had to bury something in the garden. I was grateful it did not involve a black cat, as my black cats were always the first to go missing, as their blood or bits of their anatomy were often used in spells.

Our trip to England went ahead as planned, and I was beside myself with excitement at the thought of seeing my grandmother and having the church blessing. We arrived at Mum's house in the early afternoon and almost immediately went straight to see my grandmother, as I wanted the boys to meet her. When I saw her in the old people's home she lived in I was horrified. She was in bed and unconscious and although I told her I was there, I do not think she heard me. She looked tiny and shrivelled up, her face sunken in without her teeth, and I couldn't stop crying. I went back the following day, hoping by some miracle she would be better as I so wanted her at the blessing. She seemed a bit brighter and I sat on the edge of the bed, leant over and took her in my arms.

"Is that you Linds? Is that you? Are you really here?" she said in her lilting Welsh accent. She whispered, "I'm tired now. Please hold me. I want to go home. I just want to go home." I hugged her, "I'm here Rene. It's me, it really is me." I struggled to speak through my tears.

She died during the night, the day before the blessing. The family comforted me by saying she had waited to see me, but it was no consolation, I was heartbroken. I wanted her at the blessing and I couldn't bear to think she had spent the last five months wondering why I had not contacted her.

The blessing went ahead as planned. It wasn't a massive affair, there were only forty family and friends, and the reception was not in a hotel, but back at Mum's house. Dany gave me away and Alberto was Danilo's best man. It was a strange mixture of emotions. I was sad as neither my father nor grandmother were there. Dad would have been so proud seeing Danilo in his Air Force uniform, and my grandmother had only been dead for a day. I somehow felt I shouldn't be there either, maybe I should have died too when I was shot. On the other hand I felt incredibly happy to be marrying Danilo all over again and in many ways it felt more real being blessed in church than married on the beach. As I walked up the aisle he was waiting at the altar, and in true Dominican fashion he stretched out his arm and shook my hand in greeting, which caused titters in the congregation. The vicar blew his nose as we were about to start and put his handkerchief in his pocket. Danilo was appalled, turning to me and saying in Spanish, "How on earth can he stand there with a pocket full of snot?" In the DR people blow their nose between their fingers and throw it on the ground, which I suppose is equally disgusting to us.

The service was, of course, all in English, with Danilo saying the vows after the vicar in his broken English. Mind you, he had to say, "repeat plis," a few times. We went back to Mum's house for a hot lunch of various casseroles with rice and plenty of wine. Danilo made a speech, in English, saying thank you to everyone for coming and although he was sad neither my father nor grandmother were there in person, he knew they were there in *espiritu*. That caused a few handkerchiefs to come out,

I am afraid the boys drove my mother mad. She would buy fruit for a week and they were so taken with English fruit they would be typical Dominicans and eat it all straight away. She could not understand if there was food in the house, why they had to eat it all. They would sneak out of their bedroom at night and raid the fridge, and the freezer too.

They had a brilliant time in England though, adored the dishwasher, which they had never seen before, the shops, the weather and both fell in love with the teenage daughter of Mum's next door neighbour. We all returned to the DR in good spirits.

As well as working in the *colmado* a couple of days a week, I was now giving private Spanish classes to a range of people which kept me busy, and ensured my Spanish improved. I was limited in what I could do as my voice would only work on a one to one basis, so I couldn't teach to large groups.

We decided we had to do something about the boys. The guesthouse was a tip and they often had their friends over. They were skipping school and not focusing on studying and as Dany was eighteen and Alberto sixteen, they needed to be qualified to do something. Dany was becoming lazy and arrogant and would answer me back. He was nowhere near as helpful as Alberto. But Alberto continued to 'borrow' things from our house. Danilo felt Dany needed more discipline and enrolled him in the Air Force academy, where he boarded. There, as well as discipline, he would get a good education and a chance of a good career. Alberto wanted to be a baseball player and we decided to send him to baseball school in Consuelo, a small town the other side of San Pedro. At least we were trying to give them the opportunity for a decent career.

I must admit it was a relief when they left. Fewer things disappeared from the house, and although I was pleased to see them when they came home once a month for a couple of days, life was a lot less stressful without them, and without having to clear up after them. I wanted them to have a good future, but every time we had tried to help with their education, they didn't follow it through. They went to English classes but left after three or four sessions. We had sent them to a private school, not the top of the range, but better than the standard state school, but they did not study and failed exams. I could give them the opportunities but could not make them take advantage of them.

I had tried to adopt the boys a couple of years previously, and we had provided all of the paperwork. We had been for interviews, I'd had psychiatric tests to check I was sane enough to be a mother, the children had also been interviewed. Unfortunately, when the adoption service moved offices they lost all our paperwork and said we would have to start the application process again. As Dany was nearly eighteen by then, it was going to be too late. The boys were disappointed as they wanted to have an official English mother, but on a day-to-day basis it made no difference.

Danilo continued to be involved in politics and there were several meetings in the house between him and José Luis Bencosme, who had been one of the witnesses at our wedding. José Luis was friends with the *Diputado* from San Pedro, José Maria Sosa. I suppose *Diputado* is the equivalent of one of our Members of Parliament in the UK. The whole county of San Pedro had six *Diputados* in all and José Maria Sosa was one of them.

It had been decided to split San Pedro into two and appoint a new Mayor for what was to be called the Municipality of Guayacanes, which was to be made up of seven towns and villages. The largest was Guayacanes, a fishing town where the population was mainly Dominican with some Haitians and a few foreigners. It was on the beach, and there was talk of it being developed into more of a tourist area. The second largest, in terms of population was Los Conucos, a shantytown away from the beach, but where many people lived who worked in Juan Dolio. There were many more Haitians here, but also many Dominicans. Third was Juan Dolio, where we lived, which was the major tourist centre in the area, but over the last few years it had been heavily developed with the construction of large apartment blocks on the beach, owned primarily by rich Dominicans from the Capital. There was a large Haitian population, mostly working in construction, and more expatriates. The final villages were mainly Dominican and in the countryside. They were more like *campos* (Dominican villages) with not much, if any, electricity or water. People would go to a central well for water and use gas lamps for electricity. They were called Hoyo del Toro, H3, Los Solares and Honduras.

José Luis wanted to be *Sindico* (Mayor) of Guayacanes and had promised Danilo a good job within the *ayuntamiento* (council offices), if he was appointed. There were lots of meetings in our house and Danilo tried to raise support for him. Unfortunately, it was up to the President himself to appoint the Mayor and he chose a long time senior Party member, Raoul Custodio.

Raoul Custodio did not live in the municipality, but in San Pedro. Each municipality was given money for employment, roads, municipal police, and local projects, as well as receiving taxes from the area. For example, taxes from all new construction projects, taxes per new bathrooms built, were levied in order to build a sewage system rather than relying on septic tanks. The money flowing into the *ayuntamiento* of Guayacanes was staggering.

Custodio mostly employed his friends from San Pedro in the council. He bought luxury houses and a pineapple farm. He already owned a television station and was able to develop it. The municipality of Guayacanes stayed much as it was before. The roads were mostly dirt tracks, many places had no electricity, no rubbish collection. There were no improvements in street lighting and no new jobs created for the people who lived in the municipality. And as José Luis had not been appointed, Danilo was not expecting to get the job he had been promised.

However, one of the *Regidores* (councillors) who worked for the municipality spoke on Danilo's behalf with Custodio and he appointed Danilo as Colonel of the Municipal Police. This was great but unfortunately only lasted four months as Custodio paid him once in full, the next month only half pay and after that never again. Danilo resigned.

The political involvement was not affecting me until I was in the house one afternoon. Danilo was not there, and three large *jipeta*s (SUVs) pulled up outside the gates. Out climbed ten men, mostly dressed in black, and knocked at the gate. I went to the gate nervously, and they asked to come in and see the garden. I had no idea who they were, so before I let them in I phoned Danilo.

"Danilo, there are men here. Lots of men. Where are you?"

"I come now. He important man. Let him in and say I come now. And be nice with him, he José Maria Sosa. I come in ten English minutes." I let the men in.

One of them was a little portly, with grey hair, probably in his early 50s, and he introduced himself as José Maria Sosa. I shook his hand and said, "Pleased to meet you," as he dispatched the men in black to various parts of the garden. They went onto the roof terrace and in the house, all over the place. I sat down on one of the garden benches with Sosa trying to remember I had to be nice to important people, but I had no intention of fawning over him, as the Dominicans would have done. I had no idea why he and all his personal dwendies were in my garden.

"So you need to cook breakfast," he said to me.

"Errr right," I answered, completely in the dark.

"We need boiled *guineos* (bananas) with salami and onions."

"For how many people?" I asked.

"250 to 300," he replied calmly. At three bananas each, that was up to 900 bananas to be peeled and boiled. The guy was crazy and I still had no idea what he was talking about. Thank goodness Danilo and José Luis turned up and did the appropriate fawning over Sosa and showed him the house and garden, and then at last Sosa and his dwendies left.

I sat Danilo and José Luis down. "Explain boys," I demanded. It appeared Danilo had agreed with José Luis that Sosa could use our garden and house for a party for his supporters. Although he was the *Diputado* for this area, he did not have a local house suitable for such an activity. It was to be for 250 to 300 people and he would provide the drink – vodka and juice for breakfast, whisky and juice for the rest of the day, a live band, and barbecued pig, rice and salad for a late lunch. The party would start at ten o'clock and finish by six. I had to provide breakfast. This was to happen in three days time.

Whilst I was cross at not having been consulted, I was upset I would have to peel and cook 900 bananas, let alone fry salami and onions. As an alternative, I agreed to make ham and cheese sandwiches for 300 people instead. Seeing as they would be washed down with vodka for breakfast, I doubted anyone would notice anyway

On the day, Rachel came and helped me. We started at seven o'clock and were ready as the first people started to arrive. It was a crazy day with my garden and house full of people. My outdoor office was turned into a place for the band, and when they started the noise was unbelievable. The poor dogs were locked in the back, with their paws in their ears, and only cheered up when I gave them pigs' snouts to eat later.

José Maria himself arrived at about five o'clock. He did the rounds of all the tables saying hello to everyone and pressing the flesh. At least he said 'thank you' to me. I thought he seemed like a nice man, very gracious and considerate.

When they left the mess was unbelievable. The pool was full of bottles and paper cups. My bathroom was knee deep in toilet paper and I will not describe the bidet. Dominican women often go to the toilet in groups and if they cannot wait they will use whatever is available. No toilet paper goes in the toilet, as we mostly have septic tanks, and there is a bin for the loo paper. Desperate women will use the bin, and as there was a bidet in my bathroom they had used it too. The whole garden was full of rubbish.

At last it was all clean, although Oui Oui was heartbroken at the mess. If this was politics, I was glad we were not too deeply involved.

I had made several friends on the DR1 website. Shirley's partner, Charlie, was back in the UK having treatment for cancer, and as she was on her own I decided to go and see her on her *finca* in the north. It was a four-hour drive, from the Caribbean south coast to the Atlantic north coast, passing through hills, plains, coconut palm plantations, from one side of the country to the other and westward along the Atlantic coastline. Danilo called me constantly on the phone to make sure I was alright. Shirley was a little older and even shorter than me, with short greying hair, and we had a similar sense of humour and chatted most nights on DR1. I had a lovely relaxing time on her farm, reading, walking down through her fields, past the sheep and lambs to the river, and at the same time managed to meet up with other expatriates I had met online through the website.

John was not like I imagined at all. Online he was hilarious and I was not expecting this quietly spoken mild-mannered northerner, although he still had a wicked, self-deprecating sense of humour. It was also lovely to meet Ginnie, who by then had had her first book about the DR published. She lived in a large house in Puerto Plata, the main town in the north, together with her English partner Grahame.

She was an amazing woman, vibrant with flaming red hair, incredibly long fingernails and a chain smoker. She spoke fluent Spanish but in a broad English accent, which the Dominicans found hilarious. Her knowledge of the country and her understanding of the culture and the people was fascinating, and following our meeting in person, we started to communicate daily via emails as well as chat online.

When it was time to come home, the car would not start and I had to buy a new battery, which was annoying. Then on the motorway a tyre blew out. Luckily that is never a problem as someone will always stop and help, and within less than a minute an ice cream lorry drew up and helped me change the tyre. When he'd finished, he drove behind me for a few miles to check I was alright.

At last I turned into the track leading to our house. I was very grateful to be home as I was dying to go to the toilet. A hundred metres before the house I met a *jipeta* coming the other way. Four men got out, drew guns and surrounded the car. I could feel myself beginning to shake.

"Out of the car," they yelled, one waving papers at me, the others waving guns. I cautiously pressed the window button so the window only slid open a tiny bit.

"*Que pasa?* What is going on?" I croaked. I am not sure if they heard me, but one of the men shoved the papers up against the window and told me he was repossessing the car. I had no idea how they could, as we had paid for it in cash.

"Okay fine, I will get out, but the house is just there, and you can have it when I get there," I said, pushing down on the accelerator and praying they wouldn't start shooting. The priority was the toilet and as soon as I drew up outside the gates I clambered out of the car and rushed into the bathroom.

The men came into the garden, went over to the concrete table by the swimming pool and met with Danilo. They explained a couple of years previously a man had borrowed 200,000 pesos (£4000) for an operation for his son. As this man owned nothing he had asked Danilo to guarantee the loan, which he did, and he used our car as security. As usual Danilo had said nothing to me. Over the past few years, Danilo had guaranteed several loans for people, usually for cars, and if the people did not pay their cars were repossessed and it caused us no problems. In this case the man had stopped paying and the only thing they had to repossess was our car, which they did. They did agree that if we paid the outstanding balance, we could have the car back, but in the meantime they drove it away. I tried to take out the brand new battery I had just bought, but they wouldn't let me.

As soon as they left, Danilo sprang into action and went to look for the man who owed the money. He found him, but this man and his family had no money at all; there was no way they could help get our car back. They did, however, have a pig and offered to give us that.

In the end we managed to come up with the money and Danilo went to pick up the car. Unfortunately, as the men were driving our car to the car pound, they had an accident and wrote it off. Danilo went to the local *fiscal* (district attorney) and together with lawyers and police managed to get the repossession company to give us a car of similar value.

I was waiting for him to come back with the Mitsubishi and he returned with a Ford pickup. It was massive, petrol and not diesel, manual and not automatic, and not four-wheel drive. At least it had no bumps or scratches. The fact it was a manual gear-box was a good thing as it meant less people would borrow it. However, those who did, who said they could drive a manual car, had no idea. They would often never change gear as they would have a cell phone in one hand and a *Presidente* beer (local brand) in the other. We were to go through three clutch systems in the next twelve months. And we never did get the pig.

Although Custodio had been appointed the *Sindico* for Guayacanes, it was not a permanent appointment. There were to be elections for a new *Sindico* in May 2010, not only in Guayacanes but throughout the country, and at the same time elections for Senators and Deputies (*Senadores* and *Diputados*).

I knew Danilo was enjoying being involved in politics, and one evening after dinner he led me to the concrete table and bench under the palm trees next to the pool.

"Lindsay," he started a little haltingly, "I want to tell you I want to be *Sindico*. I want to be Mayor."

"Why?" I asked, a little confused. "To be Mayor here you need to be very rich, or well-connected or be very high up in politics. Look at Custodio, he's a friend of the President, and on the main committees for the Party. You have no experience, no contacts, no *nada*."

"I want to be Mayor – we both want to help people. If I am Mayor we can help many peoples. Jobs, we can try and ask for a hospital, ask for an ambulance," he said excitedly. "We make roads happen and help people have electricity and water. We help young peoples have future and hope. Listen, now we always helping people with food and money and medicine, but money won't last forever. This way we help peoples for years."

It was a nice idea, to think we might be able to help so many people in such a huge way and maybe this was a way I too, could make a difference.

"Do you really think you might win?" I asked incredulously. "There's no point in wasting money on this just to play at it."

"I think I win. Many peoples like me. I know I am a *chivito* (little goat), but I think will win. Compres and me talk to many peoples and they say they vote for me."

I lit a cigarette and took a long slow drag. "So if we say yes, then what happens?" I asked cautiously.

"First I launch campaign, then the party members vote for me or Custodio, the man who is *Sindico* now, as candidate for party, and if I win we have election between me and other party. Afterwards if I win that, I Mayor."

I had no real idea as to what was involved, but as he was enthusiastic and there seemed no real reason to say no, we decided to give it a try. And maybe this was the reason I had not been killed. Maybe I was supposed to help Danilo become Mayor and we could make a difference to thousands of lives. It could be quite exciting.

THE DOMINICAN REPUBLIC IS A REPRESENTATIVE DEMOCRACY. The President appoints the cabinet, executes laws passed by the legislative branch and is Commander in Chief of the armed forces. The President and Vice President run for office on the same ticket and are elected by direct vote for four-year terms. There is a Senate with 32 members (*Senadores*), one for each province, and a House of Representatives with 178 members known as Deputies or *Diputados*.

Each province is divided into municipalities – 155 in total, and each municipality has a Mayor or *Sindico*. The Mayor is in charge of the town hall (*ayuntamiento*) supported by a group of councillors known as *Regidores*.

There are two main political parties – the PLD, *Partido de la Liberacion Dominicana* (Dominican Freedom Party) and the PRD, *Partido de la Revolucion Dominicana* (Dominican Revolutionary Party). In addition there are a host of smaller parties, the largest being the PRSC *Partido Reformista Socialista Cristiano* (Dominican Social Reform Christian Party)

There is not a clear left or right political division between the parties, both have slightly different policies although it is said the PRD supports the poorer elements of the society and the PLD the more wealthy.

Elections for the President, Senators and Deputies, and Mayors are held every four years. They used to be held in different years but it was decided to bring them together. In 2010, elections for all positions other than President were held – each position to last for a term of six years. The Presidential election was then held in 2012, and in 2016 there will be elections for all positions and every four years thereafter.

San Pedro de Macoris is a province with one Senator and five deputies. It was divided into 5 municipalities and it was decided in 2008 to subdivide the municipality of San Pedro itself into two – San Pedro and Guayacanes, bringing the number of municipalites in the province to six.

The municipal elections are held in two parts. First the primaries are held, when members of the same party vote to choose the candidate to represent their party at the public elections. There are primaries for each of the main parties. The winners of the primaries faced off against each other in the main election in May 2010.

CHAPTER SEVEN
A NEW DREAM

ONCE THE DECISION WAS MADE WE GOT TO WORK AND FRANKLIN Compres was appointed as Danilo's political adviser. This was the same Franklin Compres who looked like Bluebottle and was a witness at our wedding. Danilo had to register as a candidate with the Dominican Liberation Party (PLD), we had to arrange for business cards, flyers, posters, baseball caps, flags, and make plans to officially launch his candidacy. There was excitement in the air, and I was enjoying getting back into the world of work, rather than just teaching Spanish and helping out at the *colmado*.

Compres formulated the plan and I arranged for the printing and production of the merchandise. Danilo had his photo taken and the strap line was chosen, '*Danilo para un municipio seguro*', 'Danilo for a safe municipality'. There were several reasons for choosing this as the campaign slogan.

Firstly, there was no hospital in the municipality, and many people had died due to the lack of medical facilities and ambulances. Secondly, there were often robberies, especially in the relatively rich area of Juan Dolio, and expatriates did not feel safe. Also there were many people living below the poverty line with a lack of basic sanitary conditions, responsible for all sorts of illnesses. We rented a venue for the campaign headquarters on the main motorway through Guayacanes. This would be used for the launch and as headquarters during the campaign. This was the first part of the planning Compres was responsible for, and, as with all of his subsequent plans, it was vastly under budget. I was responsible for raising money and paying suppliers. No one would do any work for potential politicians as they were renowned for never paying, but for some reason they trusted me as I was English. They believed English people would pay. Which I always did.

The whole area of finance was very important as other than my pension and a small amount from the *colmado* and the Spanish lessons, we had no income. Danilo had to resign from the Air Force, as it was not allowed for a member of any branch of the military or police to be involved in politics.

"Danilo, where do you think the money is going to come from?" I asked him one morning.

"Once we launch money will come in," he promised me confidently.

"Yes, but where exactly will it come from?" I persisted. "Who is going to fund the campaign? And how much will it cost?"

"People who want me to win. Lawyers, constructors, business people. And the *Junta Electoral* (Electoral Court) will give party money and they give to me when I official candidate. No worry, the money will come. We don't need use your money."

He seemed very confident and I was sitting next to him when he was talking to lawyers and businessmen who promised 200,000 pesos, £4,000, as soon as he had launched the campaign. There were others who promised the same. However, we needed money immediately to cover the launch. I decided to approach my family and friends, many of them knew what we were trying to do and I could repay them once the launch was over and the anticipated funds came pouring in.

Since leaving England I had been writing a monthly e-mail to eighty-five family and friends back in the UK, telling them about life in the DR – they were aware of the problems and the levels of poverty. Many had met Danilo, either in England or when they came to stay, and they liked him. When I had lived in England I had always helped friends or family financially whenever they needed it, and fortunately, when the situation was reversed, they were prepared to help out with funds, and we were able to continue planning the launch. I was enjoying the work and beginning to use my business brain in a way I had not done since I left England.

The day of the launch was arranged for the last Saturday in May, the day before Mother's Day. In the weeks leading up to the launch, Raoul Custodio, the existing Mayor, became a frequent visitor to the house and as a member of the same political party, he and Danilo would be running against each other in the primaries for the party nomination. Custodio was a short, portly man, partially bald and a little lighter in colour than Danilo and I thought he was probably in his late 40s. He usually wore suits and was always pleasant to me. He was accompanied by a man called Marcelino, who had been friends with Danilo for several years.

Marcelino was a confident and well-known Dominican in Juan Dolio, buying and selling various businesses. In fact it was his *colmado* we had bought a few years earlier. He seemed to make and lose fortunes quickly. Each time he sold a business, and they were always bars, restaurants, *colmados*, he would take everything with him, all the wood, toilets etc, and they would be transported somewhere else to make yet another bar or restaurant. He had also owned the local car wash and we had many political meetings there, but he would change political parties every few months, usually because he felt he was not getting anywhere. Custodio made him head of the Fire Brigade (*Bomberos*) in Guayacanes and Marcelino became one of Custodio's men and the main contact between him and Danilo.

At these various meetings Custodio asked Danilo to withdraw from the primaries, which was no surprise, as he wanted to continue as Mayor and didn't want any competition. In his mind the primaries were over and done with and no one had a chance of beating him. He would insist there was no way Danilo could win and it was a waste of money him trying. We were sure Danilo would win – the consensus on the street was Danilo had the majority of the votes in the bag. The more he asked Danilo not to run, the more concerned Custodio was becoming. I was not present at these meetings – I wasn't allowed – but Danilo would repeat what had been discussed afterwards.

One night I was sitting in my outside office, under the palm leaf roof, chatting away online, and Danilo was fifty yards away sitting at the table next to the pool with Franklin Compres, Custodio and Marcelino. It was a week before the official launch and I was surrounded by hats and posters, leaflets, and flags.

It was a beautiful evening, warm and still, the inky black sky covered with twinkling stars and the garden full of fairy lights. Custodio and Marcelino got up to leave and I waved as they passed me. Having seen them out, Danilo came into the office and sat down next to me.

"He wants me stop Mayor, and says he give me money to stop," he announced.

"How much money?" I asked.

"He says he give us one million pesos," Danilo replied flatly.

"Twenty thousand pounds? What do you think? What do you want to do?" I asked him.

"Whatever you want my love," he said smiling. "If you want stop, we stop and have money."

"Do you think you can win?" I asked.

"Yes, I know I win. I be Mayor and you First Lady. But if you want money, we take money and stop." It didn't take me long to respond. "No, let's carry on, if you're sure you can win." An enormous grin spread over his face and he got up and went back to Compres sitting by the pool.

The day of the launch arrived and the house was chaotic. There were people coming and going and I felt nervous, having no real idea what was happening. It was scheduled to start at three o'clock, and at two the *motoconchos* began to arrive outside the house. Soon there were a hundred or so. I had no idea what they were doing, but each was paid a hundred pesos for his fuel and issued with purple Party flags. They thronged on the dusty track outside the house with more cars arriving all the time, people coming in and out. They were given purple 'Danilo' hats and 'Danilo' badges. I wasn't sure what I was supposed to do and sat at the table outside watching the comings and goings. Danilo eventually came up to me and said, "You go now, I come later."

He gave me a quick peck on the cheek and I walked outside and got into the car, along with a group of other people I didn't recognise. The back of the Ford pick-up truck was full of twenty people squashed in and we drove slowly with the *motoconchos* in convoy, their flags streaming out behind them, honking their horns, down to the headquarters in Guayacanes three miles away, holding up the traffic en route. Over two hundred people were waiting there. I had a lump in my throat when I saw them and walked through them, greeting people and shaking hands.

This was my first lesson in how political campaigns in the DR were run. The candidate never arrives until after everyone else and at four o'clock Danilo turned up. The crowd, which had by then increased dramatically, went wild. Everyone was screaming and chanting his name as he made his way up to the platform where there was a long, top table. I was sat at one end, next to Danilo's sister, who I had no idea would be there, along with various party dignitaries. It was not particularly well organised. A lawyer on the top table was drunk and fell asleep, and the microphone did not work very well. Danilo's sister became concerned and turned to me and said, "I'm worried about him speaking. He should have had training for this. He has no idea. I'm worried he will make a fool of himself." I smiled and looked at her, "Don't worry, he'll be fine. He knows what he's doing."

I knew Danilo had a photographic memory and had no need of notes, and once you put a microphone in his hand he went back to the time he worked as a DJ on the radio. He stood up to speak, smiling and showing the gap between his front teeth. While I could tell he was nervous, as he kept blinking, once he opened his mouth his confidence increased and he spoke fluently. He told the enthusiastic crowd he would try to get a local hospital built, put pedestrian bridges over the motorway, provide an ambulance for the area, and he would increase the size of the police force to fight crime. He planned to set up a market where people could sell their produce.

The crowd yelled in support each time he mentioned another item on his agenda, as journalists present took notes, and photographers took pictures. There was a raffle for liquidisers, irons and coffee pots – it was Mother's Day the following day, another reason why we had gone so far over budget, and there were the usual scuffles from the women, fighting over the winning tickets. There were two bands scheduled to play, Michael Jackson, the Guayacanes version, and a rap singer called *el Funky*. We left after *el Funky* finished.

I was to learn the Candidate arrives, speaks and leaves quickly. We were mobbed as we were leaving, with people asking for money and shoving medical prescriptions into our hands. The car was covered with people, trying to get close to us. I had never seen anything like it as I was bundled into the car. We arrived back at the house and more people began to turn up, congratulating Danilo, who kept asking me if he had done well. I assured him it was fine and the next day even the national press reported on his launch. The level of excitement started to mount and I waited for the money to come pouring in. Danilo did manage to raise some, but the majority of the wealthier people still did not think he could beat Custodio, so funds were not as substantial as we had hoped. Nevertheless we carried on working.

There were *mano a mano* – literally hand to hand – when we walked through the streets in various parts of the municipality shaking hands, and the people would give us a list of what they wanted – zinc sheets for the roof, bags of cement to help build a house, concrete blocks, bags of sand, always medical needs.

Frankin Compres trotted alongside Danilo writing down what people wanted in a notebook. It quickly became apparent people voted depending on what they were given, not with their hearts, and not with what they might get in the future. For the vast majority it was not about manifestos, it was all about 'give me now'. I thought if they preferred Danilo, if they liked what he was trying to do, they would vote for him. The reality, for the majority, was what we could give them now. If we thought their vote was secure, we would return later with what they had asked for.

In the meantime I carried on raising money from family and friends. I even approached my ex-husband and although we only communicated once a year to say hello and keep in touch, he was happy to help towards the campaign. We would go through times when we had enough for events such as a *san cocho* (stew) at a local bar, where Danilo would make a speech, or present baseball shirts to kids' teams, or buy the zinc or whatever people wanted. However, on the domestic front we were broke. There was no birthday celebration for Dany in the August, nor for Danilo or I in the November. Every peso we had went towards the campaign.

Danilo did not stop working. He was out almost twenty hours a day, every day. However, things were looking good and a poll put us well in the lead, and inside sources told us Raoul Custodio was becoming very concerned.

Besides Custodio and Danilo there were another three candidates. One was José Luis Bencosme, but it was obvious Danilo had significantly more support than him. He was helping the *Diputado* from San Pedro, José Maria Sosa, with his campaign to be Senator, and under instruction from Sosa he withdrew and told his handful of supporters to support Danilo. Sosa needed all the votes he could get if he was to become Senator, and he could see the groundswell of opinion favouring Danilo, and knowing how much the local people disliked Custodio he threw his support behind us. We had the key people on our side and all was looking good.

On a Thursday in September I was riding my *pasola* back from teaching Spanish, and I had a call from an American friend called Dana. I stopped the *pasola* and fished my phone out of my pocket, "Lindsay, you have to help. Ezequiel is in jail." Her boyfriend, Ezequiel, was number two dwendy. I was not too concerned, as like many people he was often being taken to jail for nothing.

"What's he done this time?" I asked.

"I have no idea, but your car is in jail too," she replied. That got my attention and I called Danilo to sort it out. He answered the phone straight away.

"Danilo, Ezequiel is in jail with our car."

"I know. Everything is okay. I will fix," he replied, confidently.

I wasn't too concerned as I knew he would sort out the issue and I carried on with the day as usual, going to our *colmado* and chatting with Rachel there, visited another friend and arrived home at four o'clock. Danilo was in the pool. I wandered over to him and crouched down by the side of the water. "What is going on with Ezequiel and the car?" I asked.

"Is a little problem, but I sort. Everything be okay," he answered, hoisting himself out of the pool. He wandered inside to dry off and put on some clothes, while I sat on the edge of the pool, kicked off my flip-flops and dangled my legs in the clear blue water, wiggling my toes.

Three large *jipetas* pulled up outside the gate and a dozen or so men got out. They were armed with shotguns and automatic rifles.

"Danilo! El *candidato*, come outside the gates!" they shouted, as they milled outside in the street. I sat there staring blankly at the gate in shock. I stood up shakily and went towards the gate cautiously, with my heart pounding. I had no idea who they were or what they were doing there. I hid behind a massive rubber tree near the gate and shouted out as strongly as my voice would allow,

"Who are you? What do you want?" The one doing the shouting yelled back, "Coronel... ".

I didn't catch his name, but I knew it meant police colonel.

"Tell Danilo to come out," he yelled at me.

"I don't know if he is home," I shouted back in a raspy voice. "I have only just come in. I'll go and see if he is inside." I scurried off into the house trying to hide behind trees and pillars on the way in case they shot me. What the hell was going on? I went into the bedroom and Danilo wasn't there. I ran from room to room, looked under the beds, in the cupboards, but there was no sign of him anywhere. The Colonel was repeatedly yelling, "*Candidato* come outside. Don't be a coward, come outside *candidato*."

I went to the window in the bedroom, which was near the gate, and shouted as loud as I could, "He isn't here. He isn't at home." They stood in a huddle talking and then most of them drove off but two stayed outside the gate. There was no one in the house but me. Oui Oui was in the *colmado*, and Dany and Alberto, who were home for the weekend, were nowhere to be seen. Strangely, there were no dwendies and no visitors. I was to find out later there were police stationed at each end of the street stopping everyone from coming near the house.

I waited and waited. There were no phone calls and no visitors. The house and garden were eerily quiet. *Where on earth did Danilo go?* I wondered. *Where did he disappear to?*

Why didn't he say anything to me? I called his phone over and over again. No answer. The phone was switched off. I began to feel uncomfortable and scared. And where were the boys? In the end, at eight o'clock, I called Poché, a police friend of ours, and asked him to find out what was going on. He called me back within minutes. "Danilo has been taken to the capital for investigation," he said grimly.

"Investigation? What the hell for?" I asked.

"Narco trafficking." My heart sank, and I started shaking. The one word which fills your heart with dread. Drug dealing. The worst thing. Being caught with only a tiny bit of marijuana was a long jail sentence. If you were charged with dealing you would lose everything and be sentenced for years.

"Impossible!" I said firmly. "No way would Danilo be involved in anything like that."

But it was true. Danilo had been taken to the DNCD (Drug squad) headquarters in the capital for investigation and was being held there. He had not been arrested, he had been detained. And I had no idea why, or what had happened.

I was completely alone in the house and terrified as to what would happen. There was only one sentence for drug trafficking, at least twenty years in jail, and I was sure Danilo had done nothing wrong. He had been set up.

I couldn't eat or sleep, all I could do was answer the phone as people started to call, and the phone didn't stop ringing. Everyone wanted to know what was going on. As I had no idea I gave no information to anyone, not knowing who to trust. Custodio called and offered his help, as did the other candidates, but I had no idea if one of them was behind it. In the end I phoned Saya, number one dwendy, who had disappeared, (Saya would always disappear at the first sign of trouble) and he told me the boys were at a friend's house, and gave me the name of Danilo's lawyer, who I called immediately.

It appeared that when Danilo had gone into the house to get changed, he knew exactly what was going on and had already arranged to meet his lawyer and the *fiscal* (district attorney) from San Pedro. He had climbed over the back wall of the house and run through the woods to meet them, while the police were talking to me at the front gate. The three of them had driven to the local police station from where Danilo and his lawyer were taken to the capital. He had not said anything to me so as not to worry me.

I stayed up all night terrified the police would come back and arrest me. I told no one what was happening other than Ginnie in Puerto Plata. She knew a lot about politics in the DR and it was good to have someone to talk to. She agreed it was a set up, to cause problems for Danilo as the elections were getting closer. Nobody came near the house during the night, but as the sun rose I noticed the police had disappeared from outside. At seven o'clock I switched on the local news stations on the radio and television. All of them reported the pre-candidate for the PLD had been detained in connection with drug dealing. The lawyer called and said he was sorting it out but he needed money and we arranged he would come over in the evening. The day dragged.

A couple of people came over – Chi Chi, Danilo's half-brother Antonio, who had recently moved to Juan Dolio to help with the campaign, and the boys finally returned home. I found out more people had been detained at the same time as Danilo. Four of the dwendies were in jail in Juan Dolio, and two of them had been shot and injured. My car was impounded. Compres was apparently being held with Danilo in the capital. Again, I didn't go to bed and the lawyer finally arrived at two in the morning. He said he was confident he could get Danilo out of the DNCD headquarters, but of course needed money. Fortunately, earlier in the week my brother had sent some money for the campaign, and I used this to pay him.

Saturday passed in the same way as Friday. A little group sat on the patio talking including Chi Chi, Antonio, Dana, and Prieta, Compres' wife.

"Lindsay, you have to go to the capital and see Danilo. You have to take him food, as you know they don't give you food in jail," argued Antonio.

"I can't go," I replied. "Danilo always said if there were problems I should stay out of the way. I have spoken to Ginnie, and she agrees with me. If we have to pay a bribe it will be much more if they see I am foreign. And he doesn't want me involved in problems. I just can't go."

"Don't go Lindsay," said Dana. "There won't be anything you can do," she added.

"But someone has to take him food," Antonio persisted.

"Well, you go," I said. "I'll give you the bus fare and money to buy him food and you make sure he's alright. I'm praying they don't hurt him... I just can't bear it." I bit my lip hard trying not to break down. Antonio went but he was not allowed to see Danilo, although he was promised Danilo would be given the food.

By the time Sunday arrived I was beside myself. How much longer could I cope with not knowing what was happening? At last the lawyer phoned to tell me Danilo was being released to the *fiscal* (district attorney) in San Pedro, who subsequently declared Danilo had not been charged with anything, was innocent of all allegations against him, and that it had all been a mistake. Some mistake. Danilo called me from San Pedro,

"I coming home. Everything is okay."

I felt the tension of the past few days pour out of my body and began to relax for the first time. Suddenly the empty house began to fill up. The people who had stayed away began to reappear. By the time Danilo came home there were over a hundred people in the garden. He arrived in a car driven by the lawyer, accompanied by Ezequiel and Compres. They looked tired and dishevelled but were unharmed. One of the guys who had been shot was carried in and laid on one of the concrete benches. Everyone milled around asking Danilo questions, saying they had been at the house the whole time, concerned for him. There had been no one here at all.

Danilo walked up to each one, shook their hand, and beckoned me to the bench near the pool where we sat down and he told me the story.

A few weeks previously he had been approached by someone asking if he wanted to buy a house. It was on the other side of the main road and Danilo thought I would probably like to move to somewhere with no memories of being shot. As he loved to give me surprises he agreed to buy it.

On the fateful Thursday, Danilo sent a couple of dwendies to the house to change the locks, as it had recently been broken into. He went there himself, together with Franklin Compres. Danilo left and a few minutes later a large group of armed police turned up. They arrested the two dwendies who were changing the locks, handcuffed them and forcibly threw them face down on the ground. The policemen put a gun to their heads and yelled, "Danilo is selling drugs from here isn't he?"

"No way!" they replied, terrified. "We just came to change the locks."

The police calmly shot both at point black range in the back of their legs and said, "You were shot while running away.

We will ask you again. Danilo is selling drugs from here, isn't he? If you do not give the right answer, the next shot will be through your head."

The two dwendies, face down in the dirt, one bleeding heavily as he had been shot through the knee, and the other through the calf, naturally agreed with the police.

The police went through the house and found Compres and another member of the team, Barani. They were also threatened with guns to their heads, and arrested. Compres and Barani were taken to the DNCD (Drug Squad) headquarters in the capital, one dwendy was taken to the local police station and one was taken to hospital under guard as he was bleeding heavily.

The police came to my house looking for Danilo. Fortunately I wasn't there, nor was he, but just as Ezequiel was taking the car out to fix it, he and the car were arrested. The police searched the entire house, illegally, as they had no warrant, and left.

When I returned home and saw Danilo, he was aware of everything that had happened, and also knew the police and DNCD had been paid to kill him. It was to appear as if he were a drug dealer, shot in the back to look as if he were killed running away. Danilo called his lawyer and the local prosecutor (*fiscal*), arranging to meet them and go with them to the police station. That way the police could not find him alone in the house and kill him. When the police arrived outside my house, whilst I was there, they were desperate to get him outside to shoot him, while he slipped over the back wall and through the woods to meet his lawyer and the *fiscal*.

From the local police station he was taken to the capital and interrogated by the DNCD. It was obvious there was no case against him and after the maximum seventy-two hours investigation, they either had to charge or release him. They had no alternative but to release him.

The *fiscal* said the new house would be retained by him for the time being. Danilo was not too concerned about this as he was grateful to be free and we had no intention of moving there straight away.

He showered and changed and left with a huge group of supporters to walk through the streets of Guayacanes. Everyone could see he had been released and Danilo wanted to let the people know it had been a political set up and he was still the pre-candidate.

The next day, together with the others who had been arrested, Danilo went to the *fiscal* intent on issuing a *querella* (writ) against the police who had shot the two men. However, the *fiscal*, Abraham Ortiz, would not accept it, and the police colonel agreed to send the offending policemen to a different station. We had our suspicions as to who was behind this as it was clearly politically motivated.

In the meantime, one of the men who had been shot, Hector, was in my spare bedroom. Dominican custom dictates if someone is working for you and is injured you have to look after them, financially and sometimes physically. I had paid the lawyer to get each of the dwendies out of jail, 5,000 pesos each (£100), and also paid the medical bills for the other injured man, although he had not been too badly hurt. Hector, however, had a massively swollen knee with stitches in both the entry and exit wounds. Luckily, the bullet had missed the kneecap by a fraction so nothing was broken. We paid for x-rays and consultations and he was told to be immobile for six weeks – in my spare bedroom.

I took him dinner one night, pork chops, and he looked at me, horrified.

"Are you trying to kill me?" he asked, with a look of shock and surprise on his face.

"No, why?"

"Everyone knows if you eat pork when you have been injured, you will die." I had never heard that gem of Dominican medical practice, but Danilo and the rest of those gathered for dinner confirmed it, and were astounded I did not know. I decided to conduct an experiment and asked Hector if he would like sausages instead, which he readily agreed to, of course not realising they were pork sausages. Surprisingly, he did not die.

We continued campaigning hard for the next six weeks. The posters were changed to say *'Para que votar por otro, si Danilo es de nosotros'* 'Why vote for another, if Danilo is one of us' which went down very well and seemed to resonate with the voters more than the previous slogan.

The next major event was held in Guayacanes on a Saturday afternoon. Each of the Party candidates for *Sindico* and *Regidor* (councillor) were introduced to the crowd and handed their certificate endorsing their nomination to be a pre-candidate. It was an opportunity for the supporters of each candidate to attend, and for people to see who had the most support. Given what had happened there was a chance our support would have dwindled dramatically, so we were nervous beforehand.

We started off at the campaign headquarters on the main road and marched through Guayacanes. The number of people taking part in the march was incredible, with Danilo and I at the head. There were drums and everyone singing, *'Danilo pa' ayuntamiento'*, 'Danilo for the Town Hall'. As we walked through the narrow streets people came out to watch, or waved from windows or rooftops. More and more joined our ranks. We arrived at the bar where the event was being held, accompanied by five hundred people.

There was no sign of Custodio or his supporters. Matos, another candidate who was currently in third place, had twenty supporters or so, and *Pelo Fino* (fine hair), the final candidate, had the same. There were twenty candidates for *Regidores* as well. The five *Regidores* receiving the most votes in the primaries would proceed along with the winning candidate for *Sindico* to the next round, which would be the main election in May. The primaries were very important to them too.

Each of the candidates took their seat next to the party electoral representative running the proceedings. Each would be announced, make a short, one minute speech and be presented with their certificate. It began with the *Regidores*. There was still no sign of Custodio. Once they had finished, the party representative decided to continue and announced Danilo. All hell let loose.

Custodio entered with five strapping bodyguards and a group of thugs who were shouting and pushing and banging on drums. They overturned the top table and the party representative ran away. We were carried and pushed outside and hauled onto the roof of a nearby house into relative safety. It was chaos. Danilo's supporters were shouting his name and we stood and waved from the rooftop. There was no way we could continue, so we scrambled down the back of the roof and left. We did manage to get Danilo's certificate, but it was a shame the day had not gone according to plan. Speaking to the press the following day, Danilo said he wanted a campaign which was fair and disciplined, and he felt it had been too dangerous to continue with making a speech. We continued campaigning hard and tried to think of new and innovative things to do.

Danilo and I were working together all the time to make sure he won. With his understanding of the Dominican people and the country, and my links with the USA and Europe and previous business experience, we thought we should make real progress. While he pursued his plan to build a hospital in Guayacanes, I was canvassing Canadian doctors to send a group to train the local Dominican doctors in emergency medicine.

Danilo also wanted to do something special for the families and children and an English friend of mine, Laura Jane, together with her Dominican husband, ran a circus company in the east of the country and they performed at hotels in the resorts of Punta Cana and Bavaro. I talked with Laura Jane and she agreed to put on a free show for us, suitable for children and families. Whilst we wanted to hold it in Guayacanes, where most people lived, there was not a suitable venue and we decided on Los Conucos, the second biggest town in the municipality. Held at the baseball stadium, we arranged for lighting to be installed and hired five hundred plastic chairs. Buses were organised to bring people from other parts of the municipality and 'Michael Jackson' was asked to perform again. We also invited José Maria Sosa to come along and he agreed.

The day of the circus arrived. There had been posters up for over a week and a truck driven around with loudspeakers announcing the day and time of the performance. I was a little worried not many people would turn up. It was due to start at six o'clock, in daylight, but the fire show towards the end would be in darkness and therefore more spectacular.

As usual, nothing went according to plan. Generators wouldn't start or ran out of diesel, and the lighting wouldn't work. In the end we started an hour late, with the lighting working at last. Over five thousand people turned up. It was incredible, and hearing all of those people shouting Danilo's name brought tears to my eyes. The MC shouted out, "*Para que votar por otro?*" "Why vote for another?" and the crowd shouted back, "*Danilo es de nosotros*", "Danilo is one of us."

José Maria arrived and was astonished by the number of people. He raised Danilo's arm in the air and shouted, "This is your next *Sindico!*" and once again I felt a big lump in my throat, – I felt so proud and emotional. The crowd went wild shouting and singing '*Danilo por ayuntamiento*'. The circus itself was a dazzling show, and nothing like it had been seen in the area before. As it came to a close, the MC asked everyone to leave but please not to take the chairs with them. In the end only seven went walkabout.

It was a fabulous night, and everyone agreed it had been a great success. We'd had it videoed and it was screened on television the next day, and Danilo went on the main radio stations to talk about it. We carried on working day and night for the next couple of weeks up to voting day, on 28 November, 2009. A few days before the vote, one of Danilo's right hand men was deliberately run over. Luckily he was not badly hurt and only had to spend a couple of days in hospital, but Danilo decided not to take any chances.

"Lindsay, you go hotel, as is too dangerous," he announced as we sat having lunch on the patio, three days before the elections.

"No, I'm fine," I assured him. "And anyway I should be here with you."

"No," he insisted, dropping a piece of chicken on the floor for one of the cats. "The house will be very full. Many people. Many noise. No leesping. You stress here with many peoples, many noise, many mess. You go hotel."

I wasn't too pleased with the idea but I could see his point, as he had enough to do worrying about himself without the stress of worrying about me too. By now we had bodyguards in our house and with him at all times. On the one hand the hotel was lovely as I was exhausted. The food was fabulous, there was air conditioning, and it was nice to have some peace and quiet after having had such a full house for so long. And I could have a bath. But it was lonely, although I did have the Internet to keep me company. I was worried about Danilo, and of course on tenterhooks to see if we would win.

We knew we should win as the latest poll had Danilo with 75% of the vote, and what was more important was the rejection rate – people were asked which candidate they *did not* want. Custodio had a rejection rate of 68%, Matos 85% and Danilo 0%. By this stage Pelo Fino had decided not to proceed and had told his small band of supporters to vote for Danilo.

The campaign was at crazy levels with support continuing to grow. We were told Custodio was paying Danilo supporters to vote for him. As far as we could tell they were taking the money but staying loyal to us. The media were assuming Danilo had won, asking how an unknown nobody could beat Custodio, the current Mayor and a long time senior member of the Party. Buses were hired to take people to the voting station from the outlying villages, training lessons were given teaching people which box to put their cross in, as a lot could not read, and spaghetti and rice were bought to cook meals to hand out to people in the voting lines. Twenty people were employed to walk up and down the line to make sure the opposition were not buying *cedula*s (identity cards) so people could not vote. You needed your *cedula* to vote and it was common practice for the opposition to buy them from you to stop you voting. Security men were employed to travel on the buses to ensure they only picked up our supporters. Everyone was saying God was on our side and we were going to win.

Although I was stuck in the hotel, Danilo would come every night to pick up the money I was taking out of my UK bank account, thanks to very generous friends and family. He had also managed to raise some money himself, and we thought we should have enough for the last day.

Usually he would come with his two security guards. It was always lovely to see him and we would sit and have a ten-minute chat, when he would assure me all was well. He turned up again on the night before the election with the usual two security guards (black hats with 'security' on the front, black glasses, black jackets, black gloves, guns stuck in waistband and six feet tall). They were either side of him and behind him were ten to fifteen more security guards. Flak jackets, sawn-off machine guns, black hats, black glasses, black boots.

The hotel reception was open and spacious with several large seating areas, and the tourists lounging around the reception desk thought it was a war starting. They began to move nervously and quickly towards the rear of the reception area, behind the sofas, as I pottered up to him, gave him a hug and the money, and off he went.

At the time I did not understand the need for the extra security, but I was soon to find out why. Earlier in the afternoon the car Danilo always travelled in was shot at. It was covered with Danilo stickers and posters, and had blacked out windows. He would always sit in the back. It was ambushed on the back roads between two of the villages. Dany was driving and he panicked when he saw and heard the guns and crashed into a tree. The perpetrators drove off. Dany recovered, but the car was written off.

I went to bed too nervous to sleep, but finally dropped off to be awakened when Danilo rang at four o'clock in the morning. "Lindsay we need today's money. Please get money out of machine. I am downstair. I wait for you. Hurry."

I got up and ran to the lobby in my pyjamas where Danilo and his band of security guards were waiting. I handed over the money, gave him a hug and a kiss and went back to bed. I had managed to fall asleep again when the phone rang at five o'clock. He needed two extra buses ready to pick people up. I could not get money out of my UK account as I had reached the daily withdrawal limit, which the bank refused to increase. I phoned my mum and as usual she came to the rescue and went off to Western Union and sent him some cash. Back to bed.

I spent the rest of the morning quietly but was so nervous I was unable to have lunch. The phone rang again. Danilo told me he was winning in all three tables. The tables (*mesas*) were the equivalent of voting stations, but were situated in one place, at the school in Guayacanes. However, Danilo had been told the opposition were buying *cedulas* from his supporters to stop them from voting.

The rest of the afternoon and evening dragged slowly and at last at half-past eight at night Danilo called me.

"Lindsay, we win! We win, we win, we win!" He had won, he had really won. He had won with an unofficial 85% of the votes. I put my head in my hands and the tears poured down my cheeks. I could feel the tension of the last few months disappearing. At last. At bloody last.

Danilo arrived at the hotel and we went to the restaurant and ate. I was ecstatic and he was exhausted. We went up to the room and sat on the balcony. The original plan was to go out and celebrate with our supporters and I had my clothes ready to do just that.

"Is too dangerous to go out," Danilo said. "Custodio is very cross, and his people very cross."

I was not particularly concerned about going out as we were both tired. Danilo's phone rang. Custodio had thrown out the people from the election centre and gone in with a group of military men. Danilo immediately headed down there alone, as he had given his security guards the night off.

I wasn't at all happy with him going and tried to call his political team. None of them were answering their phones. They were all too busy celebrating. At last Danilo came back an hour later to say Custodio was demanding a recount and his men were saying lots of Danilo's votes were invalid. Luckily order was restored and Custodio had left.

Great, I thought, now we can celebrate and we went across the road to the casino where Danilo received a standing ovation from the local businessmen who were there. Half an hour later yet another phone call, and off he went again. Custodio insisted on five recounts and would not let the head of the voting station sign the paper declaring the result (the *Acta*) and showing the number of votes. At last the paper was signed and Danilo went to see José Maria Sosa and José Luis Bencosme in a hotel in San Pedro, where they congratulated him.

This time he got back at three in the morning with a copy of the *Acta*. He had won and the results he held in his hand made it official. Although originally we estimated he had won by some five hundred votes, the official paper showed it was only by thirteen. Nearly enough votes had been destroyed, but not quite.

The next morning Danilo left the hotel at seven and I arrived home at noon. I walked into our garden, which was full of people, all congratulating, hugging and kissing me. They were all saying *"Feliciades Primera Dama!"* "Congratulations First Lady!"

But what a state the house was in. I had been away for four days and the house and garden had been constantly full of people. I had not been present to stop them entering the house and things were missing; all of my tea towels, (Dominicans do not dry dishes, they have no idea what a tea towel is for, and I have no idea what they did with twenty tea towels), at least twenty glasses, all the toilet paper, one of my kittens, and the cat litter tray. Later I discovered my jewellery had gone, not that there was much, but it was very upsetting to lose it all.

In addition to the missing things the car had been shot up and crashed, the water pump no longer worked, so there was no water in the house, and various chairs were broken. The house and garden were a tip and there was rubbish everywhere.

Still, we had won, and there was an incredible mood of celebration.

The next day we held a press conference where Danilo thanked all of his supporters and we went to church to give thanks for the victory. Danilo was exhausted and came down with a high fever, spending the next three days in bed. There was no actual celebration, but no matter. We had won and now had to prepare for the election on 17 May against the opposition party, when all being well Danilo would be elected *Sindico*.

IN THE LAST 6 YEARS, ACCORDING TO OFFICIAL DATA 2,367 PEOPLE have been killed by the police in the Dominican Republic. The vast majority of these fatal shootings are described by the police as 'exchanges of gunfire' with criminal suspects. The police claim that the high number of such killings is a direct result of an increase in preventive policing. However, interviews with victims' families carried out by Amnesty International, and newspaper and NGO reports, suggest that in many cases police officers in the Dominican Republic fail to comply with international standards and Dominican law, and use force disproportionate to the threat they face.

In some cases, witness statements and autopsy reports contradict police claims that killings were the result of an, 'exchange of gunfire' and in a few cases, the courts have rejected the police version of events and officers have been convicted.

There are frequent allegations that some killings by police are in reality extrajudicial executions and in addition they will often shoot people in the legs, in some cases crippling them for life.

In June 2012, the people of the city of Salcedo, in the central north of the Dominican Republic, took to the streets to protest against the assassination of a member of their community who was fatally shot in the chest by the police, while on a motorcycle with his friend. (The friend was shot in the leg.) The police never offered a reason for the shooting. The community's demand for an explanation as to why he was killed was met with the utmost brutality as the National Police opened fire on unarmed demonstrators killing four and wounding more than 20. Dozens of others were unjustly imprisoned.

The National Commission on Human Rights has committed 200 lawyers, if need be, to investigate and determine, 'those responsible for the cruel, inhuman and degrading acts that not only violate the Dominican constitution but are also violations of the Universal Declaration of Human Rights as well as seven pacts and international covenants that the Dominican Republic is a party to'.

CHAPTER EIGHT
THE FIGHT GOES ON

I THOUGHT NOW DANILO HAD WON WE WOULD BE ABLE TO GET on with the business at hand and start campaigning for the main election in May. That should be a much easier battle. However, Danilo still had to be acknowledged by the party as the official candidate. He had won, there was no question, but the official confirmation was due on 13 December, only two weeks away. Unfortunately, Mr Custodio was not about to give up so easily.

The day after the election he started submitting complaints to the Party Electoral Commission. He presented one paper after another. First claiming the person in charge of counting the votes was biased in favour of Danilo. Then he said a box of votes had been found on the beach, which had not been counted. These were later found to be from San Pedro, although we had no idea how they ended up on the beach in Guayacanes.

During this time Custodio was involving the press, who have to be paid to print most of the political news, especially regarding individual candidates. Every day, in both the local and national press, there were articles suggesting Custodio was actually the winner and he would ultimately be declared as such.

This was not what I had expected. I thought he would accept he had lost. Obviously this situation was confusing the electorate as they read the papers, watched the television and heard on the radio that Custodio would be the candidate for the PLD.

At the same time as trying to change the result by contesting the legality of the election, Custodio kept sending Marcelino, the head of the Fire Brigade, to our house with offers of cash for Danilo to step down as candidate. After one such visit Danilo came up to me in the kitchen where I was cooking lunch.

"They want me to not be candidate. Custodio want me to sign paper saying he be candidate for party, not me. Do you want me to sign paper?" he asked neutrally, without expression.

"No, I don't," I said firmly, continuing to slice onions. "After all we've been through, do you think you could just walk away from this? The people want you for *Sindico*. They don't want him. They voted for you – you can't let them down now and walk away with a bag of money."

Danilo smiled ruefully. "I think so too. But it may be dangerous. He is very, very angry. He wants be *Sindico* again."

"Well, I can't see what he can do," I retorted. "You won and that's that."

"Okay. I told him I think about it, he will do nothing as he think I thinking," he said confidently. "I have to sign paper, he say, before official results come."

It didn't take long for something to happen. Danilo met with Sosa, the candidate for Senator, and Sosa's aide, José Luis Bencosme, who told him that as he had not accepted the cash immediately, Custodio and Mariano, the PLD candidate for *Sindico* in San Pedro, and friend of Custodio, had made it clear Danilo was in serious danger. José Luis took Danilo to a secret location and we understood he could come back after the results were ratified on 13 December.

At the time I was unaware of all this, as once again Danilo was giving me information on a 'need to know' basis, not wanting to frighten me. He told me he needed to go on a course for new *Sindico*s. I didn't buy the story, but was confident that wherever he was, he would be safe.

So there I was, almost alone in the house. Just me, Oui Oui, the dogs and two security guards. I felt safe enough, as it was Danilo they wanted not me, but I felt very disappointed that he had won and we should have been in the streets celebrating, visiting people and campaigning, instead of being apart.

The boys came home more often as they wanted to help with the campaign, and I warned them to be careful and to be on their best behaviour. We couldn't afford for anything to go wrong.

"It's fine if you want to move back home and help, but just don't do anything stupid," I instructed them. "And be warned, every girl will be after you as they think Danilo will be Mayor, and if he is Mayor they think you will have money. So no sex, as they will be trying to get pregnant so you will marry them. Come home if you want, but you had better bloody behave or there will be hell to pay, I promise you!" They meekly nodded their agreement and I hoped they would behave.

The 13 December date came and went. As usual in the DR everything was delayed and we were given no date as to when the results would be officially declared, although they were available online. Danilo was still in hiding and I tried to live life as normally as possible. Everywhere I went I was accompanied by at least one security guard, usually Elpidio. Elpidio is an old fashioned Spanish name, but its literal meaning is, 'he who begs'. Nice name. I never found out what his real name was. He was single with no children, which he was desperate to have as he was now in his mid thirties. If I was meeting with female friends, he would ask them outright if they wanted his baby, which was disconcerting. He was sweet enough and my constant shadow throughout the day, guarding me when I was on the computer, coming shopping with me and he told my mother on Skype his job was to stop the bullet meant for me, which made her feel better.

Throughout all of this, Mum had been incredibly supportive. She provided money to back the campaign and would talk to me every day to check how things were going. It was lovely to feel she believed in what we were trying to do.

Danilo came home before Christmas, having been told by the party he was indeed the official candidate. At the same time it was announced there could be no official campaigning until 26 January, so we had a period of relative calm. Danilo told me the *Junta Electoral*, the Electoral Court, would give money to each official candidate for their campaign, and he was positive we would be able to raise money from local businessmen now he had beaten Custodio and was the PLD candidate for *Sindico*.

We had no Christmas as we had no money. No tree, no presents. My brother sent me money to buy presents for the boys and I went into San Pedro, bought them clothes and there was enough left to buy a turkey. I wanted to make a proper Christmas lunch. It was crazy. I walked into the supermarket and someone shouted, "It's Danilo's wife!" That was it, I was mobbed. *"Dame eso, yo necesito"*, "Give me, I need", was yelled at me from all over the shop. I only just escaped with my turkey.

Throughout this period Danilo was having constant visits from the local judiciary and assistant *fiscal* from San Pedro, warning him if he didn't resign the candidacy there would be serious consequences for him and his family. But we carried on regardless and started campaigning quietly. We made house to house visits, giving presents to the children on Kings Day, 6 January (the celebration of Epiphany), and we had a meeting for the party activists, together with José Maria Sosa, where he confirmed Danilo was indeed the candidate. Danilo was out of the house most of the time. He said he was working like a prawn. Apparently that means he never slept, as if a prawn sleeps it gets washed up by the tide and dies. A well-known Dominican saying.

It was announced in the press the money from the *Junta Electoral* would be handed to the parties in March. This money was to be given to every candidate to help with their campaign expenses going forward to the main election. At least we knew now when it was coming.

My mum was planning to visit for a couple of weeks. I was looking forward to seeing her and had arranged for us both to travel to the north of the island to visit some of my friends, especially Shirley and Charlie, who was back from hospital in the UK, and John, and Ginnie and her partner Grahame. I was still chatting to Shirley and John online daily, and Ginnie and I would talk endlessly about the campaign and how it was going. It would be too much for Mum to be in my crazy house all of the time. By now people started arriving at 6am, and by mid morning there would be over a hundred people in the garden. The dogs were happy as there was always food about. Dominicans need to eat constantly, and the dogs perfected their begging skills. Oui Oui spent most of the day picking up plastic cups and Styrofoam trays.

A few days before Mum arrived there was yet another blow. It was 6am and Danilo and I were in bed when suddenly there was a commotion outside. One of the security guards came to the bedroom window.

"*Candidato*," he whispered loudly. "There is a problem. Come quickly." Danilo leapt out of bed and threw on his dressing gown. He rushed outside and went towards a group of fifteen people leaning over the table peering at one of the national newspapers.

"*Que pasa?*", "What's happened?", The group moved aside so he could see the paper. There was a major article on Figueroa Agosto, a Puerto Rican drug dealer who was in hiding in the Dominican Republic. There were always articles about him in the paper, and rumours he was associated with several different people in authority, the military or the government. The article was accompanied by an organogram, which had photographs of everyone supposedly associated with Agosto. There were fifty photos and right at the edge of the organogram was an old photograph of Danilo, from his first *cedula*. It gave his name, that he was a PLD candidate, and that he allegedly owned a house claimed to have been owned previously by Agosto. We did not recognise the house in the photo.

Danilo came inside, dressed and went straight to see José Maria Sosa, who told him to ignore the article and not worry about it, Danilo was the candidate. He said not to speak to the press although it appeared someone had been paid to provide Danilo's name to the newspaper. Whilst we were following Sosa's advice, listening to the radio station announcing yet again that Danilo was a drug dealer, Custodio and Mariano, the PLD candidate from San Pedro, went in front of the Party Electoral Commission. They insisted the party now believe them and demanded Danilo should not continue as candidate, as serious allegations against him had been published in the national press and therefore must be true.

Danilo was summoned in front of the Commission and told Guayacanes was now being put on the reserve list. This was a list of municipalities where elections had not been held, but where the Party nominated the candidate. The Commission said if Danilo could obtain a paper from the Attorney General's office stating he was innocent, and had never been investigated for being associated with Agosto he would be reinstated.

Danilo spent the next few days running around like a madman trying to get this document. He spoke to someone at the Attorney General's office, who said he knew Danilo was innocent, but he was under political pressure not to help him. Custodio was high up in the Party and had many friends in high places – his power and influence were far reaching. However, Danilo did manage to obtain a paper of Good Conduct and presented it to the Commission explaining he had been set up.

Meanwhile, Mum arrived and I went to meet her at the airport, with a lump in my throat as I saw her come through the arrivals hall. I fought back tears as I hugged her. Once we arrived back at the house she was staggered by the number of people in the house and garden, every minute of every day. She came with me as I was campaigning, visiting houses in the outlying villages. We drove up to the north coast to see Ginnie and Shirley and she, like me, was grateful to get away from the mayhem for a few days.

"Politics here is crazy," she said as we glided along the motorway, heading north.

"Yes," I agreed. "I had no idea it would be like this. I just know the local people want Danilo to win, but I wasn't expecting such traumas. Still, we're nearly there, just need to make sure the party swears him in as candidate and then the main election should be plain sailing."

Mum was enchanted by Ginnie and sat listening as we discussed the latest political shenanigans. "It's ridiculous," Mum announced. "Absolutely nothing like England."

"No, not at all," agreed Ginnie sipping her fresh lime juice. "And I'm concerned for Lindsay and Danilo that we haven't seen the last of it."

"I can't see what they can do," I commented. "Danilo was voted in as the candidate, so what can they do about it?"

"Hmm, well... let's wait and see," answered Ginnie.

We had a relaxing time staying at Shirley's farm, went to Cabarete beach to eat fantastic large plates of prawns, Mum's favourite food, and reluctantly headed home again to see what awaited us.

We assumed everything had been sorted out and prepared to go to the *Juramentacion* (Swearing in) ceremony on the Sunday. This was when all the Candidates for Senator, Deputy and *Sindico* would be sworn in by the Party, and was a major event. This was also the day Mum was leaving. We worked out she had time to go to the *Juramentacion*, and go to the airport immediately afterwards, even though it was in the opposite direction. Of course I wanted to go to the airport with Mum, but Danilo wanted me to go to his swearing in, and the swearing in ceremony would be the culmination of all our hard work.

Sunday arrived and off we went to the capital. There were three cars full of people, and we arrived at the Olympic Centre where the ceremony was being held. It started an hour late, which I suppose was not bad. We were seated upstairs and Danilo was downstairs with the rest of the candidates. There was an electric atmosphere; the place was packed with everyone wearing purple and waving purple party flags. I was surprised at how professional the stage looked. The Ministers came out – the equivalent of members of the Cabinet in the UK – and took their seats on the stage. They sat reading newspapers and talking on their mobile phones. One of the ladies was applying her make up. I thought it would start then, but first we had to listen to a couple of bands playing Dominican dance music. As always the volume was the loudest you could imagine. Poor Mum, she hated loud music and it was getting hotter and hotter. Alejandrina German, head of the party Electoral Commission, stepped forward to read out the names of the candidates who had been elected. As Guayacanes came closer and closer we were getting ready to cheer and go wild. Even Mum had her flag ready to wave.

German did not mention Danilo's name at all. We looked at each other stunned. She did say the results were on the Internet in the final bulletin issued after the elections, and of course Danilo's name was still there. But it did not take away from the disappointment of him not being acknowledged in the arena.

We were all quiet in the car on the way back to the house, and as soon as we arrived we loaded Mum's cases into the car. It wouldn't start. We tried everything, but no joy. I called a taxi instead and clambered in with Mum. I hoped she'd had a nice time, but to be honest I had been feeling pretty stressed most of her visit, and I could see she was becoming more and more annoyed with the corruption in the political system. She, together with my sister Elisabeth, and her husband, Gary, were our biggest supporters, financially and morally, so it would have been nice if things had been calmer.

We settled back for the next round in the battle. The press was making a big deal that Danilo's name had not been mentioned at the *Juramentacion*, and Custodio was claiming he was now the candidate. Danilo continued to go to the capital on a daily basis to try and get the paperwork from the Attorney General's office to clear his name. In the end he came up with a new plan and changed lawyers to Dr Odalis Ramos.

Writs were issued to the head of the DNCD (Drug squad), the head of the National Police, and the Attorney General's office forcing them to provide any evidence they had linking Danilo to Agosto, or proof he had done anything illegal. Once issued they were stamped and signed for, as received. They were required to be issued for a further three days after that. If the information was not forthcoming after that time, we could take them to court. Danilo and Odalis spent every day running backwards and forwards in the capital issuing writs.

In the meantime, Custodio's people were tearing down Danilo's posters throughout the municipality, and where walls had been painted purple with his name, they were painted over.

The writs were issued for the second time. Danilo went for yet another meeting with the party Electoral Commission, accompanied by José Luis Bencosme, Sosa's right hand man, and returning home at four in the morning. The head of the Electoral Commission told him that without papers declaring his innocence he could not be *Sindico*. But he was also told to choose who he wanted to take his place and José Luis Bencosme was suggested. He was the man who had withdrawn from the Mayoral race and had supported Danilo throughout the campaign. Now we were supposed to nominate him as Danilo's replacement candidate. It did not make sense.

Danilo wanted to be *Sindico* and if he resigned everyone would believe the rumours and accusations were true. Why should he resign because someone had lied to the press? The electorate wanted Danilo; Bencosme knew that as he had withdrawn from the race and given his support to Danilo.

The next night we were meeting with Danilo's political team when José Luis arrived. He walked up to the table where we were all sitting.

"Hi everyone," he said cheerily, as he shook our hands one by one. One of the security guards brought over a chair for him, which he pulled up to the table and then sat down.

"José Luis, would you like a drink?" I asked.

"Sure, coffee please," he answered pleasantly, and I walked into the kitchen to get it while the men exchanged pleasantries. As I walked back with his mug of coffee he pulled out a paper from his inside jacket pocket and handed it to Danilo.

"You have to sign this," he said. Danilo read it silently and wordlessly handed it to me. Everyone at the table was straining to see what the paper said, so I read it out loud.

"I, Danilo Feliz, agree to resign as candidate for *Sindico* for the PLD and appoint José Luis Bencosme in my place." There was uproar as the team howled and shouted in disbelief, banging their fists on the table.

"José Luis, I don't get it!" I said incredulously. "The people voted for Danilo, not for you! Why should he now resign and appoint you?"

"Because, Lindsay, he will never be allowed to be *Sindico*. Better me than Custodio, as I will give him a job," he replied patiently.

"But why can't he be *Sindico*? He hasn't done anything wrong, it's Custodio causing trouble all the time," I persisted, heatedly. Danilo had been very quiet through all of this, but then he turned to his team.

"What do you want me to do?" he asked them quietly. Everyone started yelling and banging the table again. "No sign anything! You are candidate, and you, José Luis, can get the hell out of this house and never come here again!"

José Luis got up and left, saying calmly, "This was your only option. I was just trying to help. The party will not let you be candidate as Custodio has too many powerful friends. He will never let you be *Sindico*." There was silence after he had gone and Danilo put his head in his hands.

"I am so fed up of this," he said, wearily. The team looked on, not knowing how to respond and Compres replied, "We just keep on fighting." I didn't understand what was going on. This was supposed to be a democratic country.

The following day the writs were issued for the final time. In the meantime Custodio contacted Odalis and offered him money to stop assisting us. Odalis declined. He asked Odalis to pass on a message to us that if Danilo renounced his candidacy and put Custodio in his place, he would give us one and a half million pesos and give Danilo a good position in the *ayuntamiento*. Danilo declined. Custodio could not comprehend it was not about the money. It was about helping thousands of people who lived in poverty and who had no hope of a future. He had been brought up in poverty, he saw it every day, and now he had a real chance to help. We both did.

We received the paperwork back from the writs and did not have to take court action. They all confirmed Danilo was innocent. He had never been investigated, he did not own a house previously owned by Agosto, and he was clean as a whistle. We submitted everything to the party who said and did nothing, still refusing to confirm Danilo's candidacy. On advice from Odalis, we decided to launch Danilo's campaign to be Mayor, as official candidate of the party, on the following Sunday, 7 March, 2010. This was to show the electorate Danilo was the candidate and to put an end to the rumours and lies being whispered by Custodio, and to force the party to recognise his candidature. If they refused to recognise it, we had time to go to another party before the official registration date at the *Junta*. We also wanted the party to see how much popular support Danilo had.

Barani, one of Danilo's best friends and very supportive throughout the whole campaign, hired us a Lexus. We drove to the launch with four security guards standing on the footboards and hanging off the side of the car – just like I had seen on TV with the American President. We arrived at our campaign headquarters, which was heaving with people. The street in front of the building, which was the motorway, was impassable to traffic as it was full of people, all wearing purple and waving flags. However, none of the senior party members we had invited turned up.

Many local people had not seen Danilo since he won the election in November and this was now March. They went wild. Danilo stood up to speak.

"I am your Candidate. You voted for me, and I will not let you down. Together we will work to create jobs, to help the young, the old, the sick. I will develop sports in the area, work with the churches and neighbourhood groups. I will win the election for you."

It was a great speech and as soon as it finished we got back into the car, Danilo perched on the roof with his feet through the sunroof and we went off on a *caravana* (a long line of cars and motorbikes), through the municipality. Everyone had flags and waved them, and we were preceded by a car full of speakers with our music, "*Danilo pa' ayuntamiento*". It was crazier than ever before. Everyone came into the streets cheering and more and more people joined the parade. Danilo really did have the support of the people.

I was hanging out of the back window, listening to the music, the shouts of the crowds, the roar of the motorbikes, and people were running up to me shaking my hand, shouting, "*La Primera Dama!*". At last I felt we were back doing something positive and campaigning with only two months to go until the elections. We waited to hear something from the Party. It didn't take long.

The next day, Danilo was out and about and he didn't get home until five in the morning. It seems people like being woken up by the candidate when they are asleep. It shows he cares about you so much he does not go to bed, and knocks on your door at three in the morning, gets you out of bed in your underpants and you are so happy he has come to see you in the middle of the night, you vote for him.

On the Tuesday, I went to work in the *colmado*. There was no sign of Danilo when I arrived home and I cooked dinner and sat down for a night on the computer chatting to friends. I heard a car pull up outside and Danilo strode in through the gate almost running to get to me. It was nine o'clock.

"Go and pack, we are leaving," he ordered.

"How long for?" I asked, knowing better than to ask why.

"A couple of days, an' hurry, there no time to waste," and he went off to talk to the security guards. I hurried into the bedroom and threw a few things quickly in a sports bag and came back outside. Frankin Compres was there, pacing up and down, smoking a cigarette.

"What's going on, Compres?" I asked him.

"Danilo will tell you later," he said. "Now hurry." He looked nervously at the gate. Danilo came over and said, "Right, we go, no questions. Do what I say." We went round to the back of the house next to the well.

"We go over wall. People watching front," ordered Danilo. He climbed up first and threw the bags over, then helped me up.

"Watch for barbed wire," he said, as he manoevered me over. He helped Compres next, who was shaking with fear. It was pitch dark, but Danilo led us through the woods, the long grass and brush scratching my legs as I tried to pick my way carefully, whilst he dragged me by my hand. On the other side of the woods Ezequiel, number two dwendy, was waiting in a car with its lights turned off. We clambered in and Danilo made me lie on the floor, while he and Compres crouched down on the back seat. It didn't take long until we arrived at the same hotel where I had stayed before. We registered and went to our adjoining rooms.

Danilo sat me on the bed and told me what was going on. On Monday night, the night before, he had been summoned to yet another meeting. He was given a paper to sign resigning and proposing Custodio as candidate.

"They told me if I no sign, you and me and the boys would be in very bad trouble. I said I needed to talk with you."

"When you say very bad trouble," I asked, "how bad is very bad?"

"Very bad," he said, slashing his hand across his throat. As usual he had said nothing to me. He and his lawyer, Odalis, went to the *Camara Contenciosa* (dispute chamber) at the *Junta Electoral* on Tuesday morning and they issued a writ against the party, demanding they acknowledge Danilo as the candidate. The court hearing was scheduled for the next day, Danilo versus the party. The reason we had to go into hiding so quickly was because there was no way they could allow Danilo to appear in court. His life was in serious danger.

"I will go in morning. You stay here and be careful. No tell anyone where you are," he ordered.

Danilo and Compres left for the court in the capital at seven in the morning, when Odalis came to collect them. I spent the day on the beach, trying to read. Once again my stomach was churning and my mind racing. The words on the pages kept blurring as my thoughts wandered. I was still there, lying on the beach watching the carefree tourists when the phone rang.

"We win, we win!" Danilo yelled down the phone.

"What does that mean?" I asked, cautiously.

"We win. I am candidate!"

I was ecstatic and went running back to my room to go online and tell those who needed to know.

As usual, when Danilo returned I discovered, "We win" could be translated as, "I think we will win." Dominican optimism at its best.

The hearing had gone very well. Odalis said he wished I had been there, and later I saw it on video. My little *chivito* was amazing. He was confident and smart. None of those named in the writ appeared in court, but the party had sent Cesar Pina Toribio, the Minister for the Government and the most senior lawyer in the country. He was up against Dr Odalis Ramos, and Danilo. He said he had only just found out about the case, but Danilo had resigned and he presented the paper Danilo had been asked to sign by Custodio on the Monday night. They had forged his signature. Danilo swore in front of the court he had not signed it, and it was not legalised.

All legal documents here are legalised by a stamp at the time they are signed. This was not. One of the judges in the court said if Danilo had resigned it would be the first time in the history of the country an elected candidate had resigned. In addition, Odalis had all of the responses to the writs confirming Danilo had done nothing wrong and the article in the national press was a fabrication.

Danilo and Compres were on a high, but we still had to wait for the official ruling from the court. They were told it would be published on Thursday, the next day, so we did not have too long to wait.

We sat on the hotel balcony in the morning, listening to the radio. It was reported that everyone was looking for us. I was supposedly in England and Danilo in Barahona. They sent people to the house to find us and the press set up camp outside the gate.

Nothing came from the court on Thursday, and during the evening we were visited in the hotel by a friendly Colonel from the secret police, who advised us both our phones were tapped. Custodio's chauffeur contacted Danilo to warn him Custodio had said that even if Danilo won the case it was not over. It never would be over until he, Custodio, was made the candidate.

We waited and waited for the result of the court case. Each day was a different story. One day we were told the result was ready and everyone went to the court in the capital to wait for it to be announced and then nothing. Custodio was constantly on the radio saying he was the candidate. The press started reporting Danilo had resigned.

We ended up leaving the hotel on the Friday. Every day Danilo and Odalis went to the *Junta* to wait for the ruling. They were told every day it would be ready the next, and the reasons kept changing. It was waiting to be typed. It was ready but the judges had not signed it. The weekend came and went. They went in again on the Monday, and on the Tuesday. It was going to the wire as all candidates had to be officially registered at the *Junta* by Wednesday at midnight. There were only twenty-four hours to go.

Tuesday night I was about to go to bed and Danilo was still waiting at the *Junta*. Just before I logged off the computer at eleven o'clock, I decided to check the *Junta* website one last time. It was there. Danilo's result was there. It was a long document, and I decided to start reading it at the beginning. I was shaking from head to foot and could hardly control the mouse. I blew my whistle to get the kids to come and read it too and decided to read it first before calling Danilo. It was very well written and explained exactly what had happened. It declared Danilo innocent of everything, and finally, at last, it ordered the party to recognise him as the candidate. There was no recourse of appeal for the party. He had to be the candidate. At last. I called Danilo.

"The result is out," I yelled as best I could down the phone.

"I know!" he yelled back. "I have it here in my hand, and I win! We win, I am candidate! I come home now. You wait for me!" He sounded jubilant. I was too excited to go to bed and began calling and emailing people. Ginnie was over the moon too, as she had been following this every step of the way. By now it was midnight and I went and put on my pyjamas and waited for Danilo to come home. A bad move as visitors started to arrive at the house. At first it was a trickle, and then more and more arrived. By the time Danilo got home there were over a hundred people in the garden. Cheering and going crazy. It was a madhouse.

The following day Danilo went to register as the candidate at the local electoral office. This had to be done by midnight. There was one form to complete for each candidate. Surprise, surprise, Custodio had paid one of the local officials to take the only form for the PLD and register himself. There were no other forms available, so Danilo could not register. There followed a week of more court appearances, more money for Odalis, more running backwards and forwards to the capital, more stress. Danilo had to get papers from here, there and everywhere, and he and the lawyer were either in the capital, or San Pedro, or the local electoral office in Guayacanes. Custodio was doing the same, and tensions were rising.

By now Danilo had four security guards with him at all times, and I had two. We also had security guards at the house. I was not allowed out, and once again it was crazy time. I felt like I was on the set of a movie.

In the end the *Junta Electoral* (the Electoral Court) sent a paper to the local Electoral office in Guayacanes instructing them to register Danilo. At last, after a nail-biting week it was all over. Danilo was the candidate for the PLD. Custodio was not the candidate, and he had lost. Danilo was registered at the main *Junta Electoral* and we had only six weeks to go until the 17 May election day, when he would be up against Johncito Hazim from the other main party, the PRD.

We had six weeks to go and, God willing, Danilo would be *Sindico* and I would be First Lady. It had to be plain sailing now. It had to be.

ONE OF THE BIGGEST PROBLEMS IN THE DOMINICAN REPUBLIC IS corruption. It affects the daily lives of millions of people in many different ways, from petty bribery of officials, to the loss of trust in public institutions and the judiciary, to fear of violent crime. It is endemic in all areas of society. On the one hand people can bribe themselves out of trouble, from a simple traffic violation, to a charge of murder. (Like the men who shot me.) On the other hand, many lawyers will take money to help someone with their case and then do absolutely nothing. The DR ranks 129 out of 182 in the Transparency International index on corruption, and according to the World Economic Forum, corruption is the most problematic factor for doing business in the country where bribes appear to be commonplace. If someone who has money wishes to stop a competitor, or to punish someone, it is relatively easy to find someone in authority who will take a bribe.

Over recent years given the DRs strategic position between the South American suppliers and the US and Europe, drug smuggling has seen unprecedented growth, with some police, military, airport, and port personnel being involved in the trafficking activity or at the very least taking bribes to turn a blind eye.

Fights between rival gangs, or the need to silence people has also led to an increase in violence.

Even the United States State Department, recognises that while there have been coordinated efforts to address corruption, improving transparency is a priority in order to consolidate the country's democratic gains over recent years.

CHAPTER NINE
LA PRIMERA DAMA

As the official candidate, Danilo and I were expected to attend a Thanksgiving service in the cathedral at San Pedro, attended by the Vice President of the country. Later in the evening, at an event at the sports stadium, he was to be sworn in by the Vice President along with the other candidates from the municipalities in the area.

Luckily my mother had brought me a couple of nice dresses, so I had something suitable to wear to attend the service at the cathedral. We drove there in a car full of security guards and were mobbed outside and inside the cathedral by reporters from the press. Everyone was taking our photo and Danilo turned to me and said, "Look - I am more famous than Tiger Woof!"

He certainly was more famous than Tiger Woods, and as I looked at him standing next to me I marvelled at the change in the man I had married. No more jeans, T-shirts and baseball caps. Now he always wore a suit, and one of my father's shirts. No more trainers, instead, highly polished shoes. He was confident and authoritative rather than shy. But the smile was the same and his heart was bigger, if it were possible. I was immensely proud of him.

The service over, we went home to change for the evening ceremony.

"Lindsay, you need wear purple now. It is party colour, every day you must wear purple," he said, as we were changing. It was never my favourite colour, but I put on jeans and a purple top and he put on a new purple shirt with his suit and off we went.

As we got into the car park at the stadium we could already hear our music, '*Danilo pa' ayuntamiento*' playing out of loud speakers on the back of a truck, and many of his supporters were already there. They trooped inside with 'Danilo' flags and posters, and I stayed in the car park with him. When it was time for him to make his entrance we walked in together, hand in hand. The crowd screamed his name and were singing his song. I joined the supporters in the stands and he took his place at the table in the centre of the arena. It was a long table with the six candidates for *Sindico*, one for each municipality, five candidates for *Diputado* and one for Senator, José Maria Sosa. They represented the county of San Pedro. The Vice President walked in, together with the Governor of San Pedro, Alcibiades, and took his place in the centre of the table.

The Vice President made his standard political speech, how the PLD would win everywhere, and then read out the names of the candidates. There was clapping and some cheering for each one, but there seemed to be only a few supporters for each of the candidates. At the very end he read out Danilo's name. Everyone went wild. There were at least a hundred and fifty of us and we cheered, screamed and sang for over five minutes. The Vice President looked stunned. I tried to capture it on video but couldn't help jumping up and down, so the video was ruined. It was over fairly quickly after that, and we went home on a high as Danilo had now been publicly recognised by the party, and he could get on with the job in hand.

A couple of days later we went back to San Pedro as the President was arriving for a *caravana*, which the candidates and their supporters were expected to attend and participate in. We were invited to meet the President for lunch first, which was very exciting. Danilo summoned his supporters, paid for petrol and arranged for crates of water and juice to be available.

On the day of the *caravana* we set off in convoy for San Pedro and as we approached the town, Danilo stood on the back seat and raised himself through the sunroof. Our music truck was driving ahead of us, blaring out loud music. We finally arrived at the rendezvous point, which was chaotic with thousands of people and cars.

We were where we had been told to be, but could see none of the other candidates. One of our bodyguards ran off to ask someone in charge what was going on. He jogged back out of breath.

"You should be with the President on the other side of town, not here!" he panted. "Go now, we have to move fast!"

"What the hell is going on?" I asked. "Why were we told to be here and not there? Are they *still* playing bloody games?"

We left our supporters and charged off in the *jipeta* to the other side of town. Many of the roads were closed off, but we managed to get within eight hundred yards of the house where the President was having lunch. Here the road was closed again and the police would not let us drive through. Danilo, Compres and I, together with the bodyguards, climbed out of the vehicle and walked briskly up to the main gate. They would not let us in, as you cannot arrive anywhere after the President, and he was already inside. It seemed ridiculous Danilo was the candidate for the party and yet he was not being given any respect at all.

Bitterly disappointed, we trudged back to the car and lay in wait. We decided to try and join the convoy as close to the President as possible, and to turn the disappointment to our advantage. It didn't take long. After fifteen minutes the President came out in his car, sitting on top of the vehicle with his legs through the sunroof.

Saya, number one dwendy, was driving our *jipeta*. "Saya, hurry up! Force your way in there! Push those other bastards out of the way!" I screamed. "Move Saya, move," yelled the bodyguards. It was not easy as the President's car was followed so closely by the other candidates in their vehicles, there was hardly any space. And no one was giving up their spot.

There followed a crazy drive through the streets of San Pedro, with us desperately trying to get as close as possible to the President's car. The security guards were hanging off the side, yelling instructions to Saya. Danilo was flying all over the car roof as we careered in and out of traffic, and I held on to his ankles to stop him falling out. In the end we were in a reasonable position and went with the *caravana* through San Pedro for over four hours. It was very hot and very crowded, but good to see so many people supporting Danilo.

When we arrived home everyone was exhausted. Unfortunately the Ford truck, which had taken some of our supporters in the *caravana*, had broken down, another clutch burned out.

The following week was Easter when we were not allowed to campaign. Danilo canvassed people in their homes and I was desperately trying to raise money. The party money never appeared. The *Junta* were holding it and although everyone else had their share, none came Danilo's way. I went back to family and friends to try and raise more. Danilo was also appealing for money locally and was reasonably successful, as people were now beginning to believe he would win, but we had nothing like the funds available to the other candidates.

With Easter over we got back to work and the days began to fall into a regular pattern. We would be woken at six o'clock in the morning as people began to arrive at the house and the night security guard would let them in. I had to wear pyjamas as visitors would peer in through the bedroom window, which was opposite the gate. It was impossible to sleep in with all the noise so I would wander outside, having fed the cats and put the first pot of coffee on. The garden would be full of people.

Danilo would sleep through the noise until the crowd started shouting for him through the bedroom window. Sometimes *Don* (Sir), sometimes *Sindico*, sometimes *el Gran* (great one). By this time they never called me Lindsay. It was usually *la Primera Dama* (the first lady) or *doña* (lady). Once coffee was made people would wander into the house and help themselves. The head security guard would go out and buy breakfast in Styrofoam containers, usually spaghetti with a boiled egg and fried plantains. I stuck to coffee and a cigarette.

I would switch on the computer and start checking the media. There were the local and national press and blogs to read through and check, which could take two or three hours. We had a press officer, Frederick, who had set up a blog and Facebook page for Danilo, and he would arrive early so we could upload photos from the previous day to both. The blog was very successful as the local and national press could take information and pictures directly from there, meaning Danilo had daily coverage in the papers. I would print off all the coverage and put it neatly in a plastic binder and as people arrived they would come over to me to see what was being written about Danilo and the campaign.

In the meantime Danilo would be surrounded by people, never having a minute to himself. He would sit in the garden, on the concrete table by the pool and people would mill around, shouting to be heard, jostling and pushing each other out of the way.

"*Candidato, Don*, I need money for... "

"*Candidato* I think we should visit so and so."

"*Don*, have you heard about whatever."

He would try and listen to each in turn, making notes and giving instructions to his bodyguards, or Compres, or reaching into his pocket and handing over cash. Throughout it all he was calm and smiling, but in the end it was too crazy and he began to use our bedroom as his office, and a security guard would allow people in one at a time.

Every other day there was a political event. Across the country each party was assigned different days to hold events so rival groups of supporters weren't facing each other. On the allocated days we always had several events planned – a raffle, a speech, a walk through the streets, attending sporting events, giving out sports equipment.

On the alternate days we usually canvassed support by visiting people in their houses, or holding meetings at our house. We would often have events at local *colmado*s where

Danilo would make a speech, and we would all eat *asopao*, a type of soup with rice, which bore a remarkable resemblance to dirty washing up water. We would pay the bar bill for everyone and leave. Everywhere we went we had our guards. If Danilo and I went to a restaurant the customers would stand up and cheer. We could go nowhere on our own – if we did, the word would quickly spread and in no time at all a crowd would gather with everyone wanting to shake his hand and wish him luck. I started to hold my own meetings too. I would go with Elpidio and another security guard and we would meet up with the candidate for Vice *Sindica*, Arisleida, and she and I would work with the women and children. We gave mattresses to families with no beds, wheelchairs to severely disabled children, and water pumps to families with no water. Danilo somehow managed to get hold of these supplies, and Arisleida and I would deliver them and take publicity photos. Danilo would try and do some, but he often had to be in twenty places at the same time, so I would do them as well. I would have meetings with groups of women in their homes to see what their key issues were. There was tremendous poverty and many women wanted to work. Unfortunately there was no childcare. I made contact with female doctors who knew about grants available from the government for childcare projects. If we used the *ayuntamiento* money to build a childcare centre, the government would pay for the staff and provide the children with food. They would have basic schooling until old enough to go to mainstream schools, and be given all their immunisations.

I talked to solar power companies to work out how we could provide electricity to those areas which had none; to doctors in Canada about liaising with them to improve the medical services; researched buying ambulances; discussed opening schools in the evenings for adult literacy classes, and discussed ideas of apprenticeships to help youth unemployment. It was all exciting, and I couldn't wait to get started and really make a difference.

Everyone was working flat out. Danilo, as well as a Vice *Sindica*, had five *Regidors* (councillors) on his ticket who were all working hard and attending different political events too. Across the whole municipality we had *dirigentes*, (local party leaders) whose job was to organise events on a more local level, to invite people to attend and to take Danilo to homes where people wanted to talk to him. There were between one and ten *dirigentes* for each of the seven towns and villages in the municipality. In addition to them, there was also someone in charge of transport, event organisation, party liaison, and sport. They were the people who were usually in the garden every morning to get their instructions for the day.

As well as the *dirigentes*, there was a constant line of people outside the gate asking for money, or help, or selling food or ice cream. The track outside the house was always full of cars and motorbikes. Danilo was pulling further and further ahead in the polls and I was stopped everywhere I went by people saying the election was in the bag. No one had any doubts at all that we would win, it was just a question of keeping working until the day of the election. Although there were still comments in the press and on the radio about the Figueroa Agosto article, they were becoming less and less. The Ford came back with its new clutch, and I made sure I was the only one to drive it. Money continued to be an issue, and in the end we borrowed some from a loan shark in San Pedro. It was a crazy interest rate, but we would be paying it back straight after we won the election, so I was not too concerned.

At about this time we closed the *colmado*. I didn't have the time to work there and over the previous year sales had been gradually decreasing as less tourists came to Juan Dolio, and some of our bigger customers moved to other parts of the country or left all together. I was using my own money to keep the business afloat, buying stock and paying the boys wages, and we needed every penny for the campaign. It was only a temporary measure as we planned to open it again once the election was over.

The final *caravana* of the campaign was remarkable. We had over a hundred cars and several hundred motorbikes with flags, music, and everyone dressed in purple. We were joined by the Governor from San Pedro in his *Jipeta*, the Minister for Sport, Jay Payano in his, the candidates for *diputado* and of course, José Maria Sosa, as candidate for Senator. But leading at the front was Danilo, once again with Barani driving a borrowed Lexus. This time I managed to get the front seat.

We started at the campaign headquarters in Guayacanes and drove through the municipality. It took hours. Danilo was waving to everyone, security guards running alongside or hanging off the car, and me shaking hands out of the window. It was very hot and luckily there was a good supply of water and beer, and Barani was organised and had a plastic gallon container that was passed around for everyone to pee in. I decided to keep my legs crossed, as the hole in the top was very small. We made it back to the campaign headquarters where Danilo made a short speech, and then we went back to Juan Dolio.

Danilo did not want us to go back to the house, as he knew it would be full of people asking for money, and we were trying to save as much as we could for the last day of the campaign. Barani dropped us off at a cafe opposite the bank in Juan Dolio, where we ordered sandwiches and waited for Saya to pick us up in our *jipeta*. Saya had been driving it in the *caravana* and we discovered he had crashed and abandoned it to be picked up later by a recovery truck. Meanwhile the Ford truck was being used to take an injured motorbike rider to hospital. He had cut his hand when he fell off his bike, still clutching his bottle of rum. I was surprised more people were not hurt, particularly on the motorbikes as they raced along the motorway between the villages. We sat in the café unable to get home.

"Danilo, come on let's walk," I suggested, as it was only about a mile.

"The candidate, he do not walk," was the curt reply. There was a whole series of unwritten rules about what the candidate should and should not do. There were dress codes – long sleeved shirts for some occasions, short sleeved for others. Suits for some events, jeans for others. There were rules for me too. Not only to do with clothing. I was not allowed out alone, and could no longer ride my *pasola*. And the candidate did not walk.

As it was now dark I suggested we walk through the back roads as no one would see us, otherwise we would be there all night. Danilo and I, and five security guards all with their guns out. It was like a scene out of *The Good, The Bad and The Ugly*, all of us in a line, walking through the woods using mobile phones to light the way. We made it back home easily, and the *jipeta* was taken to a garage to await repairs. The Ford made it back in one piece for a change.

The opposition candidate was Dr John Hazim, known as Johncito. He was a member of one of the richest families in the country, originally from the Lebanon. He was married to Sabrina Brugal, from another wealthy family, although the two of them were not often seen together. Johncito had a large house on the beach in Guayacanes and also spent time in the capital. He was not a bad man, and loved parties with his friends and hanging out on the beach. He did not expect to win and his events were tiny compared to ours. But he and his family had money and a lot of connections. They were already friendly with the main business people in the area, especially the Vicini family.

The Vicinis were another of the influential families in the DR, owners of much of the sugar cane, and most of the land in the municipality. They were planning to build a major financial centre and hotels in Guayacanes, which would mean rehousing at least half of the local population. There had already been strikes and riots as people were evicted from their homes before they were bulldozed. Danilo had promised to help the local people to investigate who held the title to the land, and if they had to leave, to make sure they were properly compensated and rehoused. The Vicinis therefore supported Johncito.

As well as organised events, meetings in the house and going to peoples' homes, every time there was a problem it was expected we would resolve it. A resolved problem meant votes. If someone's house burned down, we rebuilt it. If people died we were expected to pay for the funeral. If people were in jail we had to get them out. If people had an accident we had to take them to hospital. Unfortunately people were dying all the time and each funeral cost three hundred pounds. When people died it was always difficult for the family to raise the money for a funeral, and usually they had to sell or pawn their possessions or go into debt using a loan shark.

The worst funeral for me occurred one afternoon when Danilo was out and someone came running to the house shouting through the gate.

"*Primera dama*, come quickly to the clinic. A little girl has been electrocuted!" Elpidio got into the car with me, and we drove the five minutes down the track to the clinic. Outside was a large group surrounding a crying woman, who was physically supported on either side by people holding her up. I walked into the clinic and approached the doctor in charge.

"What's happened?" I asked.

"She was electrocuted. She went up onto the zinc roof of the house to adjust the television aerial and an overhead electric cable blew onto the roof. Once she touched the aerial she couldn't let go. No one knew what to do, they just stood watching her," he said grimly.

"Is she alright now?" I asked, horrified.

"No. She is dead. Do you want to come and see her?"

"I'd rather not," I replied hastily, and went outside to comfort the mother. I put my arms around her. "I am so sorry," I said, choking back the tears.

"She only eleven years old," she sobbed. "Only eleven. Why it happen? Why God, why? Lisabeth, Lisabeth!" she howled.

"I will take care of everything," I confidently promised, hugging her tightly. "Don't worry about the funeral." She hugged me back and I walked back inside to talk to the doctor.

"What happens now?" I asked. He looked up from his notes, "I have called the coroner who will certify death. You need to go and get the coffin and bring it here to take her to her home."

Elpidio and I went to San Pedro to buy the coffin and pay for the funeral for the following day at two in the afternoon. However, the next morning the family called and asked us to bring the funeral forward to noon and then to eleven o'clock, as the girl's body was decomposing rapidly. The poor child had literally been fried on the roof.

I went back to see the family a few days later, and again on the ninth day as was customary. It was heartbreaking and I was determined when Danilo won the election we would start an educational campaign to prevent people being electrocuted, as it happened far too often in the DR. No one had any idea what to do, how to move someone away from the source of the electricity, or how to perform CPR. General thinking was you had to cut the electrocuted person with a machete and make them bleed, then the electricity would come out of the body with the blood.

Two weeks before Election Day the final poll came out. Danilo was in the lead with 65% compared to Johncito with 34%. There was a third candidate for one of the smaller parties, Jesus Garcia, and he decided to withdraw, telling his supporters to vote for Danilo. What was equally important was the rejection rate at 41% for Johncito and less than one percent for Danilo. However, we were still waiting for the official list of candidates to be published by the *Junta*. Every day I would check the Internet, and every day there was nothing. I would not be happy until I saw Danilo's name in print somewhere.

In the meantime, Custodio had a meeting with Danilo and his team, and announced to the press that they were all one party and he was supporting Danilo one hundred percent. He told his supporters to vote for Danilo and offered his personal support. I must admit I was glad I was not at the meeting. To see Danilo shaking hands with the man who had caused us so many problems sickened me.

"How can you shake hands with that man?" I asked him incredulously. "After all he has done?"

"He knows I win now," Danilo said. "Best to be friends with me now. And that is *politica*. One day enemy but now all is forgotten. Now friends."

At last, on 6 May, the candidate list came out from the *Junta Electoral*. It was on the Internet and published in the main national newspaper. And there it was in black and white – PLD candidate for Guayacanes, Danilo Feliz. What a relief it was.

The following day we had a *bandereo*, (a *bandera* is a flag), and our supporters were outside the campaign headquarters, on either side and in the middle of the motorway in Guayacanes. We stood and waved the flags at passing cars. Seemed very strange to me, but it was well attended and no one was run over. In fact, lots of cars joined in by sounding their horns in support. It was fun and apparently an intrinsic part of the final week of the campaign. We walked through the streets of Guayacanes waving the flags and, as usual, escaped rapidly afterwards, being mobbed by people asking for money and help.

Johncito had a *bandereo* planned for the next day, but it was cancelled – our team believed it was because he knew he would not have much support. Everyone was becoming more and more confident we would win as each day went by.

We were constantly getting press coverage, and every day they reported something we had been doing. We very rarely saw anything referring to Johncito. I was therefore surprised one day to read an article with Johncito quoted as saying he was scared Danilo and his team would cause violence. There had been no trouble whatsoever during the run up to the election, and as the *Junta* had issued the schedule of who could hold events on which days, there was no chance of the two sides coming together and clashing.

Danilo worked harder and harder. There were more and more meetings with the party in the capital and San Pedro, and these usually happened late at night. He was now up at six in the morning and rarely in bed before three. I was on the go all day, running to the shops for more zinc sheets and more bags of cement, having more meetings across the municipality, especially the outlying villages. My phone rang constantly and Danilo now had four phones, which were constantly ringing. Our phones were apparently still being monitored and Danilo would get a new number each week so he could communicate without being listened to.

And a week before the election all hell broke loose.

Danilo had been to the capital to pick up a truckload of sports equipment including basketball equipment, boxing gear, baseball bats and gloves. He and his guards drove back and went to Guayacanes to unload it, ready for it to be distributed over the next few days. In the meantime, I was at a meeting in Los Solares, together with Arisleida. She and I came home and began preparing dinner, waiting for Danilo to come back so someone could drive her home to Los Conucos.

As we were sitting down to eat spaghetti bolognese the cars drew up outside and Danilo rushed in with his guards and screamed at me, "Lindsay, get in the house now! Move! NOW!" We ran into the house and a security guard came in and hastily closed the shutters.

Apparently as they finished unloading the sports equipment a group of opposition supporters in a *colmado* started throwing rocks and bottles at a truck playing our music. It was our day for events; we were allowed to play our music. The guys in the truck phoned Danilo to tell him what was happening, and he and his team immediately drove over to them. The same people in the *colmado* pulled guns and tried to kill Danilo, shooting at him repeatedly. Danilo was rapidly bundled into the car by his guards, while still being shot at and dodging hurled bottles and rocks. Three people were shot, all bystanders walking past the *colmado*. Danilo did not know if they were alive or dead. None of our people were hurt, but the car was badly smashed up. All the windows, including the windscreen, were shattered and the car was riddled with bullet holes.

The security guards rushed around our house checking the perimeter wall. They would jump out from behind pillars with sawn-off shotguns. It was like something out of a movie, and although I knew I should be scared, it seemed so preposterous, I couldn't stop giggling. Danilo called the police and an army of police arrived to protect the house and me. He went with his team to the police station to make his report. In the meantime, I got hold of our press team and within the hour we had a report written, together with photos of the cars, on Danilo's blog.

The next day the media and press were full of the incident. Some reported it as the attempted murder of Danilo, others said that our side had initiated it. Strangely enough, the press who said we had started it were those who had printed the article the week before, where Johncito was quoted as being concerned about violence. The three injured people also had differing accounts. All three were from the opposition party, but two, who had minor wounds, said Danilo's team had shot them, and the other said it was their own side, the PRD, who were responsible.

I was just grateful Danilo was alive. But the incident had obviously been planned, given the press article and the journalists who had been present at the scene – they knew something was going to happen.

The following day we were scheduled to have a large event in the park in Guayacanes, with a raffle, and to hand out the sports equipment. Our team wanted to cancel it as they thought everyone would be too frightened to attend. Danilo insisted on going ahead, and bulletproof vests duly arrived. I assumed they were for him and me but no, they were for the security guards.

"How do I put it on?" I had asked Danilo.

"Is not for you and not for me," he replied. "Is for security men."

"But what about us?" I asked, worried.

"We need show people we brave. We no wear vest," he answered me, confidently.

Off we went to the event. We were mobbed as we arrived and surrounded by security the whole time. There were over a thousand people, and it was good to see the support. Police were everywhere, on the roofs with their sawn-off shotguns, and Danilo was surrounded by bodyguards. We survived.

We were nearly at the end. There was one final event, the campaign closing ceremony, due to take place on the Thursday before Election Day on the Sunday, and after that no political activity was allowed. It was to be held in the park in the middle of Guayacanes and would be a rally with speeches and a live band. It was due to start at three o'clock, but it was pouring with rain. We arrived in a car with blacked out windows and saw people were sheltering in *colmados* to get out of the rain. I could see Danilo was very disappointed with the weather, and we headed to the local garage where we could wait for the rain to stop. Finally it did and we had a call to say the park was now full of people. Whilst we were in the garage some of the team were drinking whisky, and Danilo, who hardly ever drank, had a couple of whiskies too. I was concerned, but he said it was to make his speech better.

We arrived at the park to a rousing reception. Various people spoke and then it was Danilo's turn. He stood up confidently. "I am not a doctor. I don't have a degree. I am not rich. I am not an Arab. I am Dominican. I am just like all of you. I know what it is like to have no food, to have no money, to want a future for my children. All I ask you to do is to vote for me on Sunday, and we will work together for a better future for everyone." It was an incredible, unscripted speech – witty, amusing and from the heart. The crowd was ecstatic. The band came on after his speech and everyone was dancing and singing.

It was over, the end of the campaign. We were both exhausted and the following day I left to go back to the hotel. The next time I came home it would be as the First Lady.

DOMINICANS' ATTITUDES TO DEATH ARE VERY DIFFERENT FROM THOSE of westerners. There is usually only a twenty-four hour period between death and burial. The average Dominican does not get taken to a morgue and refrigerated, although wealthier people are taken to a funeral parlour. Once death has been pronounced, by the equivalent of a coroner, the body is placed in a coffin and taken back to the deceased's home. There a wake is held which goes on through the night.

The important components are a *carpa* (a tarpaulin) erected in the garden to shade people from the sun or protect from rain, and there is coffee and rum to drink. Haitian funerals also have drummers and fabulous singing. It is a celebration of life, although the widow and children are often hysterical, sometimes lying flailing on the floor. They occasionally become unconscious through hysteria.

The coffin has a glass window allowing the face of the deceased to be seen, and sometimes the casket is completely open. The funeral itself takes place the following day; because of the heat people need to be buried quickly. A hole is dug in the local cemetery and the coffin placed in it. If it is a nice coffin they hack it to pieces first with machetes so no one will steal it. I have never been to a burial where the coffin fits the grave, and there is often a delay to make the grave bigger, or trim the coffin or try to somehow jam it in the grave. Those who can afford it are buried in the family vault, and in this case there is no need to violate the coffin.

The family grieves for eight days and on the ninth day the coffee and the *carpa* reappear and people visit to express their condolences. They usually wear white, and once the day is over the front room, which has been turned into a shrine during the mourning period, reverts to normal and the television is turned back on.

I have been to several funerals and have often been asked to take photos of the deceased in their coffin, as few Dominicans or Haitians have a camera. I cannot say it was my favourite job, especially when it involved children, but I did get used to it. I had never known so many people die. Some were motorcycle or car accidents, which was not surprising given the standard of driving and the fact people drove cars or rode motorbikes whilst drunk, and without seat belts or helmets. Many children died of diarrhoea, due to well water being used to mix their formula. People died of heart attacks, the average diet being full of oil and salt and lacking in fresh fruit and vegetables.

Although good medical care is available in the private hospitals in the capital, or Santiago, the second largest city, the public hospitals are sadly lacking, and although they are ostensibly free, you have to pay for all medicines, which many cannot afford.

CHAPTER TEN

THE END OF THE ROAD

I LEFT HOME FOR THE HOTEL ON THE FRIDAY. ONCE AGAIN I WAS looking forward to the rest and a bath, full of excitement and anticipation now the election was nearly over. On Saturday morning Danilo came to pick up more money, and I spent the day quietly in my room or in the bar, where the Internet signal was better, chatting to people online. I could feel the tension rising and was becoming more and more apprehensive as the day went by. Everyone said we would win, we were miles ahead in the polls, but I still could not shake off a feeling of unease. I tried to picture how it would be when it was all over and Danilo was *Sindico*, but somehow the picture was blurred and would not come into focus. During the day problems began to appear. There was an issue at the voting stations; instead of an equal number of officials from both political parties, the opposing party, the PRD had far more officials than we did, which was unusual and worried me a little.

In addition to the officially appointed personnel, each candidate could nominate one delegate and one assistant for each table to ensure there was no cheating, and we had that under control. Our delegates were in place and had been thoroughly trained over the past few weeks so there would not be a problem, and we hoped they would be able to avert any potential skullduggery by the PRD officials in the voting stations.

Saturday passed slowly and in the evening I had a visit from Frederick, the head of our press team, to go through a few issues. He looked smart, as usual, in dark trousers and an open neck white shirt. We sat down on one of the sofas in the reception area.

"So, what do you think about the problem?" he asked, in a casual, off hand way, not able to meet my eyes.

"What problem?" I replied vaguely, not paying too much attention, concentrating more on lighting a cigarette.

"The problem with the ballot paper?" he persisted, a little nervously.

"What bloody problem with the ballot paper?" I asked crossly. I didn't want to hear of any problems, and what could be wrong with the ballot paper?

"Well, you haven't heard this from me, as I know Danilo wouldn't want to worry you, but he has had a letter from the *Junta Electoral*, which says 'sorry, they made a mistake and forgot to put his name on the ballot paper'. They have put Custodio's name on it, but the letter says not to worry, Danilo is the candidate."

"They've done what?" I exclaimed in disbelief, clutching the unlit cigarette in my hand. "Danilo's name was in the press, and on the *Junta* list online! How the *hell* can they forget to put it on the ballot paper? They should issue new ballot papers. Can't we get them changed?"

"Well, it's too late now. It's seven o'clock and the polls open at six tomorrow morning. They do say his photo is on the ballot paper though, and people will look at that. It's the photo we have used throughout the campaign, the one on the posters," he replied confidently.

"Yes, I know they have the photo, I have the paper here confirming they received it and confirming they'll use it on the ballot paper. Well... maybe it'll be alright, but something seems dodgy to me," I said worriedly.

At last Sunday arrived, and I woke very early as nervous as a kitten. Switching on my computer there was no Internet signal, and I dashed down to the reception area. The Internet did not connect there either. I ran to the reception desk to ask if they had a signal and they checked the main modem in the hotel. It was not working. There was no Internet in the hotel.

Meanwhile, Danilo had called me and said we needed more buses and more money for petrol to go and collect the voters. I needed the Internet to raise the money, and I ran back to the hotel reception desk.

"Please, I need to use the Internet and it's still not working. This is *really* urgent, is there any way you can get it fixed? Please?" I pleaded, stomach knotting with anxiety.

The receptionist looked at me with disinterest, "It's not working."

"I know it's not working. I'm asking if there's any way you can get it fixed," I said, trying to keep my temper.

"It's Sunday. The Internet man does not come in on a Sunday."

"Well, make him bloody come in! I need the Internet and I need it now!" I shouted hysterically, all attempts to keep my anger in check gone out of the window. "Have you no bloody idea what is happening today?"

The receptionist looked at me blankly, "Monday, it will be fixed tomorrow. Go to an Internet cafe."

I couldn't stop screaming with frustration inside and although I had been instructed not to leave the hotel, I called Dana, the girlfriend of Ezequiel the dwendy.

"Hi, Dana. Listen, there is no effing Internet in the hotel. I can't see anyone kidnapping me today, can I get over to yours and use it there? I need to find money and check what is going on."

"Sure, I'll come and pick you up," she replied calmly, and within thirty minutes I was sitting on her balcony.

I emailed all of my friends asking them to send money to my account. Unfortunately it was not going to make much difference as I had taken the maximum for the day out of the bank account and the bank would not increase my daily limit however much I begged them. Even if friends put money into my UK account I could not get it out, and it would take days to transfer money to my Dominican account. The other option was to use Western Union, but they were closed, as it was a Sunday. There was no way I could get any money from overseas. The only thing I could do was to call our friends who lived locally. Dana got on her phone and I got on mine. Slowly we started raising money.

Some people wanted to know if they would get their money back and I assured them of course they would – as soon as we won. I knew we would win as we were so far ahead in the polls, but still couldn't shake off the ominous feeling I'd had since the previous day. The day dragged on interminably.

Danilo went to vote at four o'clock. He looked at the ballot paper and his photo was not there. At least not the one we had used throughout the whole campaign, which had been submitted to the *Junta Electoral* on time. Not the one we had a receipt for. They had used a photo from his very first *cedula*, (ID) when he was eighteen-years old. There was no way you could know it was him and underneath the photo was the name of Raoul Custodio. Danilo was furious and, unbeknown to me, started to become very, very concerned and apprehensive.

At last the voting stations closed and all we could do was wait for the count. The tension was unbearable, but people kept calling me and saying of course he would win and I should stay calm. I wanted it to all be over. I felt physically sick.

I was checking on John Hazim's Facebook page, which was public. He was sitting in his house, depressed, sure he would lose. Suddenly he posted he had won Honduras. It simply was not possible. Honduras was ours, 100% ours. There was not one person in Honduras who would vote for him. I called Danilo.

"Danilo, Johncito says on Facebook he has won Honduras. He is lying, yes?"

"No Lindsay, it is true," he answered wearily. One after another the results came through. All of the places we had sewn up, Hoyo del Toro, Juan Dolio, Los Conucos – all of them for Hazim. We just had to wait for Guayacanes.

We lost every one of the six tables in Guayacanes. Every single one. We had lost at every voting table throughout the whole municipality, when we had gone into this election with a massive lead in the polls. What in the name of God had happened? It was unbelievable.

All the hard work, all the money, all for nothing. I was shaking from head to foot in shock. Dana looked at me, having no idea what to do. I stood there, white as a sheet, my heart pounding.

"I need to go back to the hotel," I said. "I need to see Danilo."

I found out later we had been attacked on all sides. Not only was the balance of officials not in our favour, Danilo's name absent from the ballot paper and the wrong photo of him used alongside Custido's name, but a host other things had happened.

Members of our party, the PLD, had been paid to vote for Hazim in an attempt to stop Danilo winning. Many people believed Danilo had stood down when his name was missing from the ballot paper. Voters did not want Custodio to win and felt pressured to vote for Hazim. And when the *Actas* appeared later, whilst the national turn out was about 60%, in Guayancanes it was 100% in some places, and higher in several others. Dead people voted for Hazim, people out of the country voted for him. It appeared there had been electoral fraud on a massive scale.

On Sunday itself, members of our own political party were outside the voting stations, including Marcelino and others who worked for Custodio. They had only feigned support for us, and were alledgedly given money by Custodio and Hazim to buy the *cedula*s from our supporters, to stop them voting. They did this all day long.

In the end Danilo had 1001 votes and Hazim 1700. There was no way Danilo could win with this kind of opposition and I was surprised, given the efforts made to stop him, that he got as many as he did.

I felt numb, shattered. Dana drove me to the hotel and I walked inside on shaky legs and slumped down on a couch in the reception area, where I broke down. I howled and howled.

Danilo was supposed to pick me up from the hotel to go and celebrate, and we were booked to spend another night there.

One of our supporters came into the hotel and walked up to me. "Lindsay, Danilo is in a terrible state at the house. He says you will leave him. He is saying he has lost everything. Come back to the house and talk to him." I pulled myself together. Whatever I was experiencing, I could only imagine how he must be feeling now.

"No, I can't go back there, I just can't at the moment and anyway I have the room here for another night. Go and get him and bring him here, please. Hurry."

I took a few deep breaths and tried to calm myself. Okay, we had lost the election, but it was not the end of the world. We owned a house and a business, which together were worth nearly three quarters of a million dollars. We could sell those, pay back everyone we owed money to, and still have enough money to go somewhere else in the country and start again. Or, as Danilo had been the PLD candidate, he was bound to get a good job with the government locally. Together we would sort it out.

Danilo arrived within minutes. He walked across the lobby towards me and I ran to him, falling into his arms, sobbing. After a minute or two we went up to the room, walking out onto the balcony where we sat down. I didn't give him chance to speak but leant forward and took both his hands in mine.

"Listen, I don't know why we lost. It doesn't make any sense, but it doesn't matter. We can sell the house, move, go somewhere else, pay back what we owe and start again. It doesn't matter, it really doesn't," I said, as brightly as I could. "It's okay. It's fine. It's just a bloody election," I rambled on. "There has to be a winner and a loser. It happens all the time." At last he spoke quietly and shakily, his voice breaking with emotion, "Lindsay, you don't understand. We have lost everything."

"Don't be silly," I replied briskly. "We have lost an election."

"No... we lost the house, the car, the business, everything... we lost everything. Everything we own. We have nothing, nothing at all... *nada*... and now you leave me and I lose you too." His shoulders slumped forward and he dropped his head into his hands, overcome with emotion.

My mouth dropped open, and I felt my heart sink and a mixture of vomit and bile rise up in my throat. "How the hell have we lost everything? The house is in both of our names! You can't have sold it because we're married. The law says I have to sign if you sell any property. I have signed nothing! How can we have lost our house and our business?" I felt the clammy sweat chill my body, and fear grip my chest in a vice.

Danilo raised his head in utter dejection and explained, "They told me all assets confiscated."

"Who told you the assets were confiscated? Why? We, you, have done nothing wrong!" I demanded, shouting at him.

"They made me sign paper to sell everything. They said if we fight they put us in jail... I go to jail but I not let you go to jail. They deport you and I never see you. They want me to resign candidacy and I wouldn't. They take everything."

"But why the hell didn't you tell me?" I stared at him in disbelief and horror at the consequences we were facing.

"Because when we win I get it back. I not want you to worry. It happen months ago. I knew we win. Everyone want me win. Everyone said they vote for me. But I no win. So everything has gone. It is all gone. Our beautiful house. Our business." He broke down sobbing. "Now you leave me. I have nothing. You have nothing. Everything is finished."

Someone else owned our house and our business. Danilo

was right. We had nothing. And we owed tens of thousands of pounds. What the hell were we going to do? I walked into the bedroom and sat on the edge of the bed, overwhelmed and unable to comprehend the enormity of what we were facing, and put my head in my hands trying to breathe. After a minute or two I walked back onto the balcony and held both of Danilo's hands.

"Look at me. When we got married it was for better or for worse. For richer or for poorer. I am proud of you. You did the best you could. You would have made a fantastic *Sindico*. But the corruption here would not let it happen. If we have to live in a mud hut, with no food, I'm staying here with you. I love you. You can't get rid of me just like that."

He looked at me with red-rimmed eyes, stunned, and eventually replied, "Now I know real love. I not know before. I never knew love be this strong. I will sort it. Don't worry, I sort everything."

We went to bed and slept as we always have throughout all of our time together, with him holding me tightly.

In the morning the reality of our situation started to hit me. We went back to the house. It was not full of people and activity like before, there were very few people and lots of tears. It was a mess. The atmosphere was appalling. No security guards, no dwendies.

I phoned Ginnie to tell her what had happened, and as usual she was very supportive. "Well, I'm sorry, but I'm glad he lost," she said.

"If he'd won, I'd have been worried all the time that they would kill him. Now you need to take care of yourself and try and get your house back. I'll send you some money now, and I don't want no for an answer," she instructed me in a very no nonsense tone.

"But Ginnie, I've no idea if I can ever pay you back," I said, with tears in my eyes at her understanding and generosity.

"Don't worry about that. I can afford to lose it and you and Danilo need it. What you both tried to do was amazing and I care a lot about both of you, so take it."

Over the next few days people brought us food. Some people still came, those few who were loyal. Everyone was talking about who had betrayed us. I had never in my life felt this depressed or angry.

The only relief from the mental anguish was when I could sleep, when I dreamed of diving, and I dreamed of being the First Lady when I felt I could have made a real difference to the lives of so many people. Every morning it was a major effort to get out of bed.

The car was taken away after a couple of days and we had no transport. We lost the *colmado* a week later, the new owner moved in and our staff there had to leave. They had no jobs and no money and there was nothing I could do about it. My partners in the *colmado*, Vic and Rachel, were furious, thinking I had sold the business behind their backs and kept the money and didn't speak to me after that. Rachel, who I thought was my best friend in Juan Dolio, never came to see me so I didn't have a chance to explain we had lost the business, not sold it. With the *colmado* not doing well over the previous year, I had lent it more money than my partners had originally paid for it, as they couldn't afford to fund it on a day-to-day basis – in reality they had lost nothing.

Danilo thought we would be able to stay in the house for a while, but I expected us to be evicted every day. One decision we had made was that we would fight back. Fight the corruption during the election and fight to get our house back.

We went to see Odalis, the lawyer we had used when we won the case earlier in the year at the Electoral Court. He said if we gave him a thousand pounds, he was confident he could get the house back, and he also believed we would have a good case to go to the Electoral Court again. As Custodio's name was on the ballot paper and Danilo was the candidate, he felt there was an excellent chance we could ask for another election. I came away feeling a little better, at at least we were doing something positive. I called my sister, Elisabeth, and she came up with the thousand pounds to pay Odalis.

We did not go out. With no car and hardly any money we could not go far, and to be honest neither of us could face anyone. The few times I walked to the local *colmado* to buy cigarettes, I would scuttle back home as fast as I could, hoping I would not see anyone. My phone was silent. Nobody called, and we had few visitors. Some friends called to see us who were selling Belgian Malinois dogs in the capital and they gave one to us, who we named Shakira, which was lovely, but most days we saw no one.

We kept waiting to hear from Odalis, but nothing. He would not answer the phone. When we did track him down he told Danilo he was sorry, but he could not help with the court case. We found out he had been contacted by Abraham, the *fiscal*, and told not to help us. He said, however, he would continue to try and get the house back. We looked in vain for another lawyer, but no one wanted anything to do with us. In the end we found one, who I did not rate, but at least he was a lawyer. He put the paper together asking for the election to be re-held with Danilo's name on the ballot paper, and it was submitted to the Electoral Court. We started to feel optimistic. There should be no way we could lose this.

The night before the court case we went to bed early. The phone rang at one o'clock in the morning and Danilo answered. "*Hola*," he said, "Why not? I thought you were our friend!" I heard him say angrily. "*Ta bien*. Alright, okay."

"What's happened?" I murmured, sleepily.

"The lawyer, he not come to court tomorrow. I need go get papers from him on *pasola*."

"Bastard. Well, we'll have to sort it on our own. Do you want me to come with you?" I asked, climbing out of bed, all thought of sleep forgotten.

"Do you want to?" he asked hopefully.

"Of course, come on, let's go," I replied, more cheerily than I felt at the idea of a trek on the *pasola* in the middle of the night. We rode into San Pedro to pick up the papers, all the time thinking how were we going to manage without a lawyer. We had no choice and when we got back we sat up until the early hours writing a speech for Danilo to present to the court, and in the morning we set off for the courtroom.

It was pretty terrifying, especially as John Hazim was there to listen to what Danilo had to say. You could see he was nervous that he may have to face another election, but chatted pleasantly enough with us. Danilo spoke well. He was clear and concise, telling the court they themselves had insisted the party put his name forward as candidate, which they had done, but why was his name not on the ballot paper? He pointed out if he, Danilo, had won, then the opposition, Hazim, would have claimed Custodio had won as it was Custodio's name on the ballot paper; either way Danilo would lose. He asked for another election on the grounds his human rights had been denied.

We left the court feeling confident and all we could do was wait for the ruling of the court. The days dragged. People still brought food, although less often than before, but somehow we managed. In the end the result came out. Motion denied. It was an administrative error and not an Electoral issue. We were gutted.

We contacted investigative journalists, the press, the Citizens Rights office, everyone we could think of. No one was interested. No one would listen to us.

Danilo seemed to be more accepting than me; I felt angry and impotent. Every day I was worried and stressed that whoever owned the house would come and evict us. The gossip was rife in Juan Dolio, just as it was after I had been shot, so we stayed at home. Neither of us could face anyone. The days fell into a regular routine. We would get up late and I would go onto my computer, but as I didn't have to check the news daily or prepare things for the campaign, I decided to write down everything that had happened to us, which became the basis for this book. It gave me something to do.

Danilo would watch television and sleep. Gone were the suits, and in fact he stopped wearing clothes, going back to his time as a child in *La Loma*, and would wander around naked, climbing palm trees to get coconuts without any clothes on. He taught himself magic tricks watching a programme on the television, and spent a large part of each day practising, which gave us something to laugh at. I stopped laughing when he needed elastic and rather than buying any, relieved all my knickers of theirs. I was grateful he did not attempt to cut me in half.

Every day something bad happened. The cleaning lady left, though I was managing to scrape the money together to pay her; her husband did not want her working for us. The gardener, Oui Oui, broke his arm and went back to Haiti, as he did not trust Dominican doctors. Between us we gardened and cleaned, it kept us busy and we could not afford to employ anyone else. We were living off my private pension, which I had taken after I was shot – it was only £500 a month and we owed so much money it made me sick to think about it.

Danilo went to visit a *brujo*, a witch doctor. The *brujo* said someone had put a spell on us and that there was a dead snake buried in our garden. Until it was found and taken away the bad luck would continue. We had to buy him a small bottle of rum and give him fifty pesos, about a pound, and he would come to the house the following Friday and dig up the snake. He did not appear on Friday – I assumed he had not yet found a snake to kill.

The children continued to invite their friends into the guesthouse. They had moved back home about six months earlier to help with Danilo's campaign. Dany had failed his exams at the Air Force Academy and been asked to leave, and Alberto was not going to make it as a baseball player as he was too thin. Obviously they both thought Danilo would win the election, and they would not have to worry about jobs, but now they needed to do something.

We did not have enough money to feed and support them, and could not afford for anything else to go missing. I would buy milk, which would disappear out of the fridge. Also Dany was back to being his usual arrogant self and in the end Danilo asked them to leave. Alberto went and stayed at a friend's but would come round every day to help me with the cooking. Dany moved in with his girlfriend. We were later to discover not only was he living with his girlfriend, but he also had a six-month-old daughter. So much for my sex education lessons. We were now grandparents and he had not mentioned it to either of us.

More bad news kept coming. Grahame, Ginnie's partner emailed me one morning to say Ginnie wasn't feeling too well and would not be online that day. I wrote back to give her my love and said we'd chat when she was feeling better. By 9pm I received another email. Ginnie had died. It was the most appalling shock and a terrible loss.

Another good friend, Charlie, Shirley's partner died of Non-Hodgkins Lymphoma, and while I was away at Ginnie's wake in the north of the island, Danilo's best friend, Barani, died in a car accident together with his wife. He was the one who had guaranteed our loan from the loan shark in San Pedro, and we had no idea what was going to happen to that.

We thought at first Barani had, for some inexplicable reason, driven off the road at three o'clock in the morning, although we were later to find out he had been pushed off the road by another vehicle. He had been murdered. It was not only a terrible personal loss for Danilo, but Barani was also a great financial support to us, especially after we lost the election, and was one of the few people who had stood by us. Danilo was concerned it was a warning to him.

For my part, I missed Ginnie terribly as she was the one person who understood the local politics. She and I would communicate every day, and she would give me advice. Most of our other friends had no idea what was going on, and only Ginnie knew about the situation with the house. I did not dare tell my mother about it, as I prayed we would get it back.

In the meantime Odalis had done nothing about the house. Of course he kept the thousand pounds saying he was working on it, and asked for more money, which we didn't have to give him. In the end Danilo found another lawyer, who agreed to work for us free of charge to help us get the house back. He would be paid when we reclaimed the house and were able to sell it. He was confident we would get it back, and told me he thought everything would be sorted by the end of November. It seemed like a long time to wait, as it was only June, although we were still living in the house and so far no one had asked us to leave.

We tried to stay positive and still hoped Danilo would get a good job, and every day he would call people, but no one wanted to speak to him. The Dominicans love winners, but want nothing to do with losers.

The days turned into weeks and the weeks into months. We were getting nowhere. One day a lawyer turned up at the gate and asked me why we had not moved out, as we did not own the house and the new owner wanted to move in. I played dumb. They were beginning to close in on us. I knew we would have to go, but I had no idea where or how, and I didn't want to leave my home. At the very least I wanted to sell it, to give us some money to start again and pay people back. It was beginning to look as if we would be out on the streets.

In the end the decision was made for us.

One Sunday morning at seven o'clock, just after sunrise, people arrived at the gate calling for Danilo. He looked out of the bedroom window and saw a crowd of police. Knowing what the police had tried to do to Danilo previously, I went to the gate in my pyjamas and he stayed inside.

There were twenty armed police together with the local public prosecutor, Abraham, who we knew. I opened the gate nervously. A brutish, overweight Colonel shouted at me, "Let us in! We need to search the house! This is the *fiscal*," he pointed to Abraham.

"I am perfectly aware who the *fiscal* is," I replied, trying to remain in control, which is not easy when one is in pyjamas. I knew the *fiscal*, having met him on a few occasions whilst trying to get people out of jail, so I turned to him.

"*Buen dia*. How are you?" I said brightly, as if this was a normal occurrence. I held out my hand for him to shake and he had the grace to look embarrassed.

"Good morning *Doña*," he mumbled, shuffling from one foot to the other as he shook my hand. The dogs were going crazy behind the gate.

"Lock the dogs up, or I will shoot them. We are coming in whether you like it or not," snarled the bloated Colonel.

"Okay, okay, *'ta bien*, keep your bloody knickers on," I snapped back. "I'll go and lock them up. Just wait here, it may take a while." "Hurry up, we need to come in quickly," shouted the Colonel.

"I said wait a minute," I retorted, "and put your guns away, I hate *armas*," and went to lock up the dogs. Danilo was in the kitchen, out of sight of the front gate. "They want to search the house, I have no idea why. What do you want me to do? Abraham is there with them," I whispered to him.

"Fine if the *fiscal* is there, they won't shoot us," he said confidently, and went outside. They came in, carrying pistols or shotguns in their hands and searched the entire house including the guesthouse. Of course they found nothing illegal, as there was nothing to find. Later Danilo went to the police station and received a paper confirming they had found nothing. He was told that apparently Custodio had sent the police colonel and the prosecutor to the house to show Danilo, he, Custodio, could do whatever he liked to us and the police and the judiciary would do whatever he wanted. Not only was it a lack of respect to raid the house of the ex-candidate, it was also a warning and gave more momentum to the gossip machine.

We had thought when Custodio saw Danilo had lost the election he would leave us in peace. It was not to be. We were told he was consumed with jealousy. He felt if he had been candidate and not Danilo he would still have been Mayor. He would not forgive us. He would never forgive us.

A couple of days later Dany was arrested by the police as he was walking in the street, held overnight and released without charge.

Next our transformer blew up – we had no electricity, and no money to fix it. At the same time Danilo and the lawyer decided to issue a writ against the paper, which had published his photo, against the National Drug Control Department and the *Junta* for everything they had done to us over the last year or so. If it was successful we might be able get our house and business back, and claim compensation.

Danilo sat me down. "Lindsay you need go away for a few days. Things might be difficult here soon, once writ issued. You need go somewhere safe. I will sort it. Pack bags and be ready to go."

"How long do I need to leave for?" I asked frowning.

"I no know. Maybe a week, maybe two week." He arranged for someone to take me away in secret, and given what had happened to Barani, I left over the back wall again, and we checked all the way to ensure we were not followed. The person who drove me was sworn to secrecy and he dropped me off a few miles from my final destination, so even he did not know where I was hiding.

I was on the north coast of the island and spent my time between Shirley's *finca*, where she lived alone since Charlie's death, and Grahame, Ginnie's partner, who was also on his own. It was a lovely break. I could sleep knowing no one would come to the gate. No one would arrest me, or worse. I was eating good food, rather than tins of sardines and plantains when we could afford to eat. Danilo had given me a new chip for my phone as both our phones were still being monitored – at least I could communicate with him. After a week he came to see me, a five-hour drive. I sat anxiously waiting, but before he arrived I had a phone call from Ezequiel, number two dwendy.

"Lindsay, Alberto has been arrested. Tell Danilo."

"Shit. What for? Where is he being held?' I asked.

"I don't know. No one knows where he is," he replied

"Well, find out and in the meantime I'll call Danilo."

I called Danilo who was only thirty minutes away from me by then. He arrived, but only stayed two minutes. Nobody could find Alberto. We had people looking in all the jails but there was no sign of him. We were terrified the police might have killed him. Danilo drove straight back to Juan Dolio and eventually located him, but again Alberto had to spend a couple of days in jail. It became increasingly obvious we, and the boys, would have to leave Juan Dolio. But where could we go?

We had fought the election with everything we had, and lost. We had lost our house, our car and our business. We had no money and no work. We owed thousands. We talked about my going back to UK, but I didn't want to. Danilo would not be able to come with me straight away and there was no guarantee he would get a visa. If I went back, what work could I get at my age and with a voice that hardly worked? And if I left the country, the place which I now considered my home, would the authorities let me back in? There was a possibility they would stop me leaving the country – we had no idea if Custodio had fixed that too.

No, we would stay here in the Dominican Republic and together we would sort it, somehow. The crisis, as Danilo called it, would have to be over soon, although it had now been five months since the elections, and in my opinion it was getting worse rather than better.

THERE WERE FOUR VOTING STATIONS – GUAYACANES, LOS CONUCOS, Hoyo del Toro and finally Juan Dolio. The last three had one voting table each, but as the maximum number of voters per table was 600, Guayacanes had six tables – there were ten tables in all.

In total 4000 people were registered to vote. The official population of the municipality was 12,000 but many of these were foreigners and not entitled to vote, or they were Dominicans who were registered to vote elsewhere.

You are registered where you had your first *cedula* or identity card, unless you made a specific effort to change it. In addition there were several thousand undocumented Haitians, and this had increased since the earthquake – they were not eligible to vote.

Each voting centre had a President of each table, a secretary and a first, second and third official. These people were appointed by the *Junta Electoral* and officially a mix of the different political parties were involved.

WHAT ABOUT YOUR SAUCEPANS?

CHAPTER ELEVEN
HOPE

───

THE QUESTION WAS, WHERE SHOULD WE GO?

We had a piece of land in Barahona in *La Loma* where Danilo had been brought up. We had bought it several years earlier and luckily it had not been taken from us. We would be safe there, and I liked the idea of living on top of a mountain, with fantastic views and pottering on a little farm. Of course Danilo had dreams of going back there as it held a very special place in his heart. But it had no electricity and no water, let alone a house, and was a good two hours drive up a tiny, steep and badly maintained track from the town of Barahona. Danilo felt it would be too remote for me.

We needed somewhere off the beaten track. Somewhere where we could live quietly and unobtrusively. I wanted to be no more than an hour or so from an airport where I could pick Mum up, if she came to visit, and an hour from a good supermarket and decent medical facilities in case I was shot again.

Danilo arranged to pick me up in the north, from Grahame's house, and we planned to travel the country looking for somewhere to live. He said once we had found somewhere we would go back to Juan Dolio until we eventually moved. At last I would be going home. Whilst I was enjoying the peace and quiet I missed my home and my cats and dogs.

He was due to pick me up at half past two, which changed to four o'clock and finally he turned up at nearly eight at night.

"So, Danilo," I asked brightly, as I clambered into the car, "where are we going?"

"We go look for somewhere to live," he answered, grinning at me.

"Well, it's dark now, so I doubt we'll find anywhere at this time of night. Where will we stay tonight?" I asked.

"In house."

"What house? Whose house? Where is this house?" I was full of questions.

"You will see," was the only answer I could get out of him, so I sat back to enjoy the ride. I had no idea where we were going, and dozed off. I was abruptly wakened with the car bumping up and down, and looked out of the window. We appeared to be in the middle of some sort of *barrio*, or neighbourhood, with lots of little wooden houses with zinc roofs. Every so often there was a bigger concrete house, sometimes one storey and sometimes two.

"Where are we?" I asked, as he drove slowly along the rutted dusty track.

"We are nearly there. You will see," he replied, smiling.

Suddenly he stopped the car, and beeped the horn in front

of a large metal gate. To my surprise Dany came running out and pulled the gate open and Danilo drove into the gravel yard in front of a two storey concrete house. And there, sat on our very own picnic dining table, were Tyson, Fred, Sophie, and Shakira, the new Belgian Malinois puppy who had been given to us a few weeks previously.

"My dogs!" I yelled, as I scrabbled to get out of the car and threw my arms around Sophie and nuzzled her neck. I was trying not to cry, but I was insanely happy to see them. The dogs were barking and jumping up at me, and Danilo pulled me by the arm.

"Come on, come inside. Come and see inside." I followed him through the front door and gasped.

"Oh my God, look!" I exclaimed. It was perfect. All of my pictures were on the walls, everything was in its place. It was spotless. Danilo and the boys had been moving us for a week. We had left Juan Dolio, never to return. Yet another of his surprises. The house was rented and had a reasonable living area, nice sized kitchen, three bedrooms and one bathroom. It also had a large fenced-in yard.

"But what about my cats?" I asked in consternation. "Where are the cats?"

"I bring them next week," he replied, grinning. Two minutes later the boys appeared with an enormous cage. The poor cats had been in there for a week. No one dared let them out as they were afraid they would escape. I let them out into one bedroom and you can imagine how pleased they were. Four had not made the journey, as Danilo could not find them to bring them. I was left with seven, but they were all fine.

Danilo took me from room to room showing me everything. It was a nice little house. The landlady lived upstairs but was leaving to go back to New York, and would not be back for a year.

"Lindsay this is where we live now until court case is over. You tell no one we are here. No one. We must be very careful." For the first time in nearly two years, I slept in my own bed with my husband, knowing no one would be coming to kill us. No waking up at every sound, no heart pounding in my chest.

Life in the *barrio* was very different. The noise for one thing. It was only quiet from midnight to five in the morning, apart from barking street dogs. The day would begin at five with the roosters crowing. The neighbours would put the radio on full blast, all different stations of course. Later the ducks would wake and the radio noise was exchanged for Dominican music from every house. At four o'clock every afternoon people would sit on plastic chairs in front of their houses and shout at each other across and up and down the street. I had no idea why they did not all sit together and talk in normal voices.

I would sit in front of the house on the little terrace writing and talking to people online. Everyone who passed would stop for a chat. Both Tyson the Great Dane, and I quickly became local celebrities. We often had a large group standing outside hoping Tyson would stand up. He was usually asleep at my feet or on the table.

We lived on my pension – £500 pounds a month. From that we paid £150 rent, plus electricity, gas and Internet, which left us with £250 for food and everything else.

There was no need to ever leave the house. The streets were full of vendors all day long. The milkman would pass by on a donkey with a churn first thing in the morning with jugs full of fresh milk for fifteen pesos (25p). It had to be boiled though, as it was straight from the cow. Little kids came round selling avocados at five pesos each or two for fifteen. Obviously they were not too strong at mathematics. There were the shoe shine boys, the shoe mending man, the dead chicken man, the baby chicks and guinea fowl man, the plastic bucket man, the scrap iron man, medicine man, coconut man, fruit and veg man, DVD man, and ice cream boys. All came on foot or bicycles, and occasionally in beaten up old vans. Everyone shouted out what they were selling. There was the fish man, the pork scratchings man, the man who carried a black plastic dustbin liner full of popcorn. It was like sitting in the middle of a market. Occasionally the washing machine man would drive past – you could rent the washing machine by the hour –which he had balanced precariously on the back of his motorbike.

The streets were dirt tracks, and it obviously had not rained for a while, so there was dust everywhere, and every morning we had to sweep the house out and mop it. Everyone was doing the same thing, all of us women sweeping and mopping, most of them singing out of tune to whatever music they had on the radio. Everyone appeared to start well before me, and I was up at seven as it was impossible to sleep with the noise.

The garden, if you can call it that, was massive. There was the main area around the house, which was mostly dust and mud, big enough to park a dozen cars in. There was a second garden, fenced off with barbed wire, which was also dust and mud. This second garden had orange, lemon, mango and guayaba trees. All had fruit when we arrived. There were several banana trees, and some sugar cane.

The barbed wire fence was perfect as a washing line and saved on pegs, though most of my clothes ended up with holes. The house came with a washing machine, which was just as well as the one in Juan Dolio had died. This one was also a twin tub, and worked perfectly apart from the spin dryer having no brake – you had to stop it by putting a stick in to slow it down. And every house had a gutter in the garden where the dirty washing water went and then flowed into another gutter in the street. I felt like I was living in Elizabethan England.

The electricity was a joke. It was off more than it was on, and was not strong enough to run my lovely double door fridge, so the fridge had to go and be replaced with a tiny one. To solve the electricity problem, Danilo had installed an inverter, a white box connected to twelve car batteries, which charged from the street electricity when it was on, and supplied us with electricity when the street power was off. It worked like a dream. We also had a generator which we could use to charge the batteries if ever they ran out.

The town was one long street, with a bank and a little supermarket and lots of small shops. There were no restaurants except one place selling fried chicken. The supermarket was small but had the basics and everything was much cheaper than Juan Dolio, in some cases half the price. I found a little market with only four stalls, but lovely fresh fruit and vegetables, and a butcher who only sold pork and beef – he had a cow and a pig a week so you needed to know which day he bought them as he often ran out. Chickens were easily available at the local *colmado*.

Life was good and I revelled in the peacefulness as each day I felt the stress leaving my body. I felt no need to go out, enjoying the calm, smiling at the neighbours and the goings on in the *barrio*. Danilo left every week to go back and meet with the lawyers, and the court date was set for the 12 November 2010. We heard Custodio was furious and trying desperately to find us. We changed our phones, cancelled our phone contracts and tried to be careful and tell no one where we were.

The plan was to stay there until we had our house back and sold. Then we could repay people and buy a little farm somewhere and start again. The 12 November date came and went, and the court case was adjourned until 4 December. More waiting. I was hoping everything would be resolved by the end of the year.

Although we were safer and life was calm, bad luck continued to haunt us. The court case was put back again until the end of January. We were getting nowhere fast. Having started off being reasonably positive once we had left Juan Dolio, I began to lose hope. We waited and waited. Days turned into weeks and weeks into months. Christmas came and went. My pension suddenly reduced by 40%, something to do with the British government thinking people would live longer and restricting how much money people could take from their private pensions. Instead of £500 a month, we had £250, which meant only £50 a month for food.

I was about to find out what it was like to be poor. There was no money for anything and nowhere to get any money from. We had no credit cards and no store cards. No money for my contact lenses – I went back to wearing glasses. None for medicines – I stopped taking my blood pressure pills and HRT. No cat or dog food – they ate boiled chicken innards. We survived on Dominican food like plantains, and started eating one meal a day. Occasionally we would have porridge. There seemed to be no way out and I would wake in the night with hunger pains and get up at ridiculous times, unable to sleep. When we were desperate I would swallow my pride and ask friends or family for help, but only when we couldn't pay the rent. If we were sick there was no money for medicine. If anything went wrong we could not fix it. We couldn't drive anywhere as we had no money for petrol. We couldn't use the bus as we had no money for our fares. I had never experienced living this way.

I hardly had any contact with my previous friends. Inadvertently leaving my telephone in a pair of jeans and washing them, I had lost everyone's phone numbers, and no one called me. The only people I had contact with were a few friends from the past, a few I had met through the DR1 forum, and my mother and sister. Danilo's friends and associates stopped calling. They were only so-called friends when he had money. Mum wanted to know when we would sell the house and in the end I told her we had no house to sell, we were fighting to try and get it back.

The court case took place, but the other side did not show up, and it was rescheduled again. Danilo explained if they didn't show at the next two hearings we would win automatically. The next hearing was scheduled for August 2011, but then there was a change at the top of the judiciary and it was changed to August 2012.

I tried to stay positive but kept reliving the scenario of what should have been. Living in a nice house, with my pool and beautiful garden. Helping the women and children in the municipality. Going out to restaurants in nice clothes feeling happy. We should have won. The Dominican music blaring out from the neighbouring houses brought back too many memories of the past ten years. Memories of dancing in bars. Memories of being happy and carefree. Having been so happy when we moved, I was beginning to become desperate for something to be resolved and for us to plan some sort of future. I asked Danilo to be straight with me.

"Danilo, will we get our house back?"

"I working on it."

"Danilo I know, but will we get it back?"

"Let's wait and see."

"Okay, let's try again. What are the chances we will get the house back?"

"50/50." In Dominican speak this means there is not much of a chance.

I accepted I would have to face reality. We were unlikely ever to get our house and business back, and I felt embarrassed we owed money to my friends and family. I was desperate to pay it back but I had no idea how to begin to repay them, with hardly enough to live on ourselves.

The dream was over. I used to see people sitting outside their wooden *casitas* and marvel at how they seemed happy although they had nothing. I was about to be the same. It had been a rollercoaster of a ride.

Do I have regrets? Of course. I wish Danilo had won, and we could have done something to help thousands of people. But it didn't work out. Not for want of trying.

My ex-husband, who lent us £5,000 for the campaign wrote to me after we had lost, and I replied asking if he could wait for his money for a while. He responded, '*At least you are living on the edge with passion, unlike the rest of us who are chasing some Holy Grail which doesn't exist.*' He hit the nail on the head. I am living with passion. I adore Danilo, even more than before. We spend a lot of time together and although I never believed we would be soul mates, because of the massive differences between us, I was wrong. Though life is hard we laugh together and share so much joy.

I am a different from the person who left England ten years ago. I left with money and now have none, none at all. I have experienced a depth of love and caring I have never known before. Not only from Danilo, but also from other Dominicans and Haitians and new expat friends I have made here. I have learned to be less selfish and more giving. The level of generosity from my family and friends has been incredible. I have learnt what is important in life are our fellow human beings – not what you are, what you do for a living, what car you drive, what house you live in, but *who* you are. The Dominicans have taught me patience, selflessness, caring, joy. I read somewhere that life can only have meaning if you learn from the past and plan for the future. But you can only be truly happy if you live for the day, for the moment.

I will definitely stay in the Dominican Republic. This is my home, my adopted country. I cannot imagine myself living anywhere else. Although I cannot deny we have had some awful times, this country is now firmly under my skin. The optimism in the face of such adversity is humbling. Every day I experience joy and laughter and come face to face with the indomitable spirit of the people living here.

Who knows what the future will bring, where we will go, what we will do. But we are fighting back. We are still waiting for the court case to be heard, which keeps being delayed for one reason or another, but Danilo says we are safe now. What is past is past. He is at university studying to be a lawyer and wants to concentrate on human rights. He says he may stand for *Sindico* in Guayacanes again one day – over my dead body! In the meantime I write my blog and work translating, writing articles and giving marketing advice. We keep our heads above water – just. There is hope, there is always hope, and whatever the future holds for us, we will face it together.

HOPE

WHAT ABOUT YOUR SAUCEPANS?

THE PLAYERS

FAMILY

Lindsay de Feliz
Danilo Feliz Torres – *her husband*
Dany Alberto Feliz Martinez – *Danilo's son*
José Alberto Feliz Martinez – *Danilo's son*
Christian Alberto Feliz Alvarez – *Danilo's son*
Diomaris – *mother of Christian*
Milena – *mother of Dany and José Alberto*
Antonio – *Danilo's half brother*
Shirley Firth – *Lindsay's mother*
Peter Firth – *Lindsay's father*
Elisabeth and Gary Eastburn – *Lindsay's sister and brother-in-law*
Peter Firth – *Lindsay's brother*
Patrick Firth – *Lindsay's brother*
Irene Jones – *Lindsay's grandmother*
Juan Feliz – *Danilo's father*
Maria – *Danilo's mother*

DOMINICANS AND HAITIANS IN JUAN DOLIO

Chi Chi – w*atchyman at rented house*
Billy – *staff at Neptuno dive and then manager of colmado*
Jason – *staff at Neptuno dive then staff at colmado*
Frank – *staff at Neptuno dive*
Araña – *gardener in Juan Dolio*
Oui Oui – *gardener in Juan Dolio*

Angelita – *cleaning lady in Juan Dolio*
Boyna – *builder in Juan Dolio*
Saya – *number one dwendy*
Ezequiel – *number two dwendy and boyfriend of Dana*
Barani – *good friend of Danilo*
Hector – *friend of Danilo*

EXPATS IN JUAN DOLIO

Klaus – *German, owner of Neptuno dive school*
Uwe – *German, staff at Neptuno dive school*
Marion – *German, staff Neptuno dive school*
Fred – *French, staff at Neptuno dive school*
Sue and Almonte – *British and Dominican owners of Freedom bar*
Rachel and Vic – *British expats*
Oscar – *Italian owner of rented house*
Dana – *American expat and girlfriend of Ezequiel*
Margaret and Terry – *American expats*

POLITICAL PLAYERS

Raul Custodio – *PLD Mayor of Guayacanes*
Marcelino de la Cruz – *Head of fire brigade and friend of Custodio*
Mariano – *PLD candidate for Mayor in San Pedro and friend of Custodio*
José Maria Sosa – *PLD Deputy and then Senator for the province of San Pedro de Macoris*
José Tomas Perez – *PLD Ex-senator for the National District, Santo Domingo – ex-Minister for Civil Aviation, ex-presidential candidate for the PLD*

José Luis Bencosme – *PLD Aide to José Maria Sosa, witness at our wedding and pre-candidate for Mayor for Guayacanes.*
Franklin Compres – *PLD Head of campaign and witness at our wedding*
Johncito Hazim – *PRD candidate for Mayor in Guayacanes*
Arisleida – *PLD proposed Deputy Mayor for Guayacanes*
Pelo Fino – *PLD pre-candidate for Mayor for Guayacanes*
Matos – *PLD pre-candidate for Mayor for Guayacanes*
Abraham Ortiz – *Public Prosecutor for San Pedro de Macoris*
Dr Odalis Ramos – *lawyer*

WWW.DR1.COM FRIENDS

Shirley and Charlie aka Whirleybird and Mr Whirleybird
Ginnie and Grahame aka Lambada and Bushbaby
Laura Jane
John aka JR Hartley

THE DOGS

Can Can – *pitbull*
Fred – *daughter of Can Can, Pitbull/ Vira Lata cross*
Tyson – *Great Dane*
Sophie – *daughter of Tyson and Fred*
Mas Guapo – *the dog that died from a gunshot wound*
Shakira – *Belgian Malinois*

AUTHOR BIOGRAPHY

LINDSAY DE FELIZ WAS BORN, RAISED AND EDUCATED IN THE UK, gaining a degree in French and German at Wolverhampton University, and an MBA at Bradford University. Following a successful career in marketing she decided to leave it all behind and follow her dreams. Walking away from an executive lifestyle, a stable marriage and the life she had always known was the toughest decision she ever made.

Arriving in the Dominican Republic as a scuba diving instructor, embracing a new life, culture, climate and language, little did she know how much impact this Caribbean island would have on her life as its people and culture drew her in.

She met and married a Dominican, becoming a stepmother to three young boys and, as she fell in love with the country and its people, became increasingly aware of the political corruption and incredible poverty endured by the majority of the population.

Shot during a burglary in her own home, when she almost lost her life, changed her outlook overnight. She and her husband determined to try and make a difference to the lives of the Dominican people around them.

Running for political office, Lindsay's husband sought to improve the lives of those in his community struggling against poverty, hunger and lack of education, often living in basic housing with little sanitation or electricity. With Lindsay by his side they were a formidable team. As his popularity grew and the campaign gathered momentum, they learned the hard way what happens to those who don't play by the rules of those in power. They could never have imagined where the journey would take them as they fought corruption and double-dealing.

Lindsay currently lives in the middle of nowhere in the Dominican Republic with her family, four dogs and seven cats.

Lindsay writes a blog about the Dominican Republic and daily life at www.yoursaucepans.blogspot.com

Twitter: @lindsaydefeliz

LIST OF PHOTOGRAPHS

CHAPTER 1

Lindsay's family in Singapore 1966. Left to right: Lindsay's twin brother Peter, Dad, sister Elisabeth, Lindsay aged 10, twin brother Patrick, mother Shirley; photograph © Peter Firth.

CHAPTER 2

The coast of Barahona 2008; photograph © Lindsay de Feliz

CHAPTER 3

Danilo and Lindsay 2007; photograph © Chris Field

CHAPTER 4

Lindsay and Danilo on their wedding day 20th May 2005; photograph © Vic Stewart

CHAPTER 5

Bullet stuck in Lindsay's back two weeks after the shooting 2006; photograph © Shirley Firth (mother)

CHAPTER 6

Oui Oui 2008; photograph © Elisabeth Eastburn (sister)

CHAPTER 7

Danilo in the caravana 2010; photograph © Frederick Nuñez

CHAPTER 8

Danilo at the Electoral Court (JCE) 2010; photograph © JCE (Junta Central Electoral) official photographer

CHAPTER 9

Danilo at the campaign closing ceremony 2010; photograph © Frederick Nuñez

CHAPTER 10

Sunset – Juan Dolio 2008; photograph © Elisabeth Eastburn (sister)

CHAPTER 11

Barrio, 2012; photograph © Lindsay de Feliz

AUTHOR BIOGRAPHY

Lindsay de Feliz, 2013; photograph © Jonathan Bayley

Also Published by summertimepublishing

BITTEN BY SPAIN

THE MURCIAN COUNTRYSIDE
– A BAPTISM BY FIRE

DEBORAH FLETCHER

… had me chuckling from the first page till the last"
Vanessa Rocchetta, Expatica.com

Available from expatbookshop.com

EXPAT FAQs

Moving to and Living
in the
Dominican
Republic

All of the things you always wanted to know about
becoming an expat in the Dominican Republic.
Plus a few of the things you didn't!

Ginnie Bedggood and Ilana Benady

"An entertaining story,
told with wit and insight"
Paul Burston, author, *The Gay Divorcee*

PERKING
THE PANSIES

*Jack and Liam
move to Turkey*

JACK SCOTT

SUNSHINE
SOUP

NOURISHING THE GLOBAL SOUL

Jo Parfitt

Printed in the USA
CPSIA information can be obtained
at www.ICGtesting.com
LVHW042318080524
779785LV00030B/566

9 781909 193314